BAYREUTH
African Studies Series

Publisher/Editor:

Eckhard Breitinger
Bayreuth University
D-95440 Bayreuth
Germany / R.F.A.

This book is copyright. No part may be reproduced by any process without written permission. Enquiries should be made to the publisher.

A catalogue record for this book is available from the British Library.

Die Deutsche Bibliothek - CIP-Einheitstitelaufnahme

Ein Titeldatensatz für diese Publikation ist bei Der Deutschen Bibliothek erhältlich.

Price per copy: DM 29.90 / EUR 14.99 (plus postage)

ISBN 3-927510-66-1
ISSN 0178-0034

© 2001 Charles Bodunde

© 2001 Cover design: Typo Grafik Bayreuth, based on Obiora Udechukwu: "Remembering Obiligbo", by courtesy of artarc Bayreuth.

Printed by D. Gräbner, D-96146 Altendorf

CHARLES BODUNDE

ORAL TRADITIONS AND AESTHETIC TRANSFER:

CREATIVITY AND SOCIAL VISION IN CONTEMPORARY BLACK POETRY

BAYREUTH AFRICAN STUDIES 58

The publication of this book was generously supported
by a grant from the
Alexander-von-Humboldt-Stiftung
in Bonn / Germany

Cover illustration: Obiora Udechukwu: "Remembering Obiligbo",
Water colour/ pencil (40 x 30 cm), 1998. Collection Steggenwenz
Obiligbo was one of the Nigerian minstrels.

To the lingering memory
of my parents:

Joseph Bodunde
&
Atolagbe Bodunde

They made paths
at dawn,
on the Earth:

His spade
spoke to the forest
and the forest became wheels…

In her tray,
the hunter's harvest
found a marketplace…

CONTENTS

Acknowledgements..vi

Introduction
Oral Traditions, Aesthetic Transfer and Critical Controversies..........1

I. Traditional Poetic forms: The Poetry of Okot p'Bitek and Christopher Okigbo..8

II. Myth, Legend and the Poetics of Heroism..............................17

III. Myth and Aesthetic Mediation: Ifa Divination Poetry and Okinba Launko's Poetry..27

IV. Oral Art Forms and Social Vision in the Poetry of Niyi Osundare and Jack Mapanje...................................... 36

V. Oral Aesthetic and the African Experience: The Poetry of Okello Oculi...48

VI. Kofi Anyidoho and the Ewe Funeral Dirge............................63

VII. Ezenwa-Ohaeto and the Masquerade Voice...........................73

VIII. The Minstrel, the Mourner and the Mask: Obiora Udechukwu's Poetry...88

IX. *Ivwie*, *Ivwri*, and *Edon*: Tanure Ojaide and the Urhobo
     Tradition..99

X.   Oral Aesthetic and the Black Caribbean Poet: Kamau
     Brathwaite and the African Image................................110

     Conclusion: Linkages and the Reading Arena..................128

     Bibliography..133

     Index..140

ACKNOWLEDGEMENTS

The major part of this book was completed between 1998 and 1999 during my Humboldt research fellowship at the Institut für Afrikastudien, Universität Bayreuth, Germany. I want to express my gratitude to the Alexander von Humboldt-Stiftung for granting the fellowship and also for sponsoring my trip to Morocco to attend the African Literature Association Conference. A good number of my interviews (with African poets) were conducted during this trip.

A version of the discussion on Okigbo and p'Bitek was published in *African Literature Today* 18 (1992). Also, a segment of the discussion on Brathwaite appeared in *Matatu* 12 (1994). I am grateful to the editors of these two journals.

I am grateful to the University of Ilorin, Nigeria, which granted me a research fellowship leave during my Humboldt year in Bayreuth, Germany.

I am also grateful to my academic host in Germany, Prof. Dr. Eckhard Breitinger who arranged those symposia and seminars that gave shape and direction to this work. I also want to acknowledge his useful information and advice on conferences, books and publishing. I wish to thank Dr. Norbert Aas for his support. I appreciate his book gifts.

I am indebted to Prof. Olu Obafemi for giving me the benefits of his vision always. Many thanks also to Joe Omoniyi, Sunday Ododo, Dr. Sola Babatunde and all the other great friends who battled for the rights of the absent.

I wish to thank those poets who granted me interview during the course of this study. They are: Niyi Osundare, Femi Osofisan, Odia Ofeimun, Kofi Anyidoho, Tanure Ojaide, Obiora Udechukwu, Okello Oculi, Toyin Adewale, Ogaga Ifowodo, Uche Nduka, Nduka Otiono and Susan Kiguli.

I acknowledge the pains borne by my wife and children during this period. Well, the study is to draw us closer.

I.

INTRODUCTION: ORAL TRADITIONS, AESTHETIC TRANSFER AND CRITICAL CONTROVERSIES

Joel Adedeji provides a working definition of oral tradition, which details the purpose and mode of its acquisition. He offers that the oral tradition is the "complex corpus of verbal or spoken art created as a means of recalling the past". For him, it is "based on the ideas, beliefs, symbols, assumptions, attitudes and sentiments of peoples"[1] and the mode of its acquisition is "through a process of learning or initiation and its purpose is to condition social action and foster social interaction."[2] The typology of oral tradition enumerated by Adedeji recognizes two main categories, namely, literary and historical types. In his classification, the literary category includes poetic genres such as *oriki* or praise and totem chants, *odu* or *ifa* divination poems and songs. This category also includes verbal formulae like incantations, parables and proverbs. The historical type includes such forms as narratives based on myths, legends and historical genres like sagas and epics. Harold Scheub makes a similar classification in his article, "Review of African Oral Traditions and Literature", where he gives the major divisions of oral tradition as "the riddle and lyric poems; the proverbs; and the tale, heroic poetry and epic."[3]

One of the characteristics of oral traditions, which relates to the nature of performance is the involvement of the community in the creative process as well as in the criticism. For instance, Finnegan reveals that in a creative performance, members of the audience neither listen silently nor wait for the chief performer's invitation before they join in. Instead, the audience breaks into the performance with their additions, questions and criticism.[4] Macebuh provides another evidence of the participatory nature of oral production. He maintains that "the farmer, the hunter, and the wine-tapper could be relied upon to muster a

---

[1] Joel Adedeji, "Oral Tradition and the Contemporary Theatre in Nigeria". *Research in African Literatures*, 2, 2 (1971): 134.
[2] ibid.
[3] Harold Scheub, "Review of African Oral Traditions and Literature". *The African Studies Review*, 28, 2/3 (June/ September 1985)
[4] Ruth Finnegan, *Oral Literature in Africa*. (Oxford: Clarendon Press, 1970): 10-11.

sufficiently meaningful response to art." They do this, Macebuh argues, "as part of their general awareness as citizens of a community of beings."[5]

Current aesthetic practices among Black artists indicate a growing interest in the techniques of the oral artists who situate their art in the African social and cosmic settings. As Mazisi Kunene argues, these kinds of settings are indeed the primary basis of all literatures.[6] The growing interest in transferring forms from the oral stock may be attributed to the writer's recognition of the functions of verbal art in society. For instance, William Bascom believes that aesthetic forms like myths and legends "contain detailed descriptions of sacred ritual, the codified belief or dogma of the religious system of the people."[7] In a similar vein, A.H. Gayton argues that the mythological system of a people is often taken as their educational system and that the children who sit listening to an evening tale under the bright moonlight are imbibing traditional knowledge and attitudes.[8] Also, in a study of education among the Chaga people of East Africa, Raum observes that there are two main characteristics, which define the people's valuation of proverbs as an oral art form. They are regarded as "inheritance from their ancestors incorporating the experience of the tribe, and they serve as instruments both for self control and for the control of others".[9]

With regards to Black art, the questions of fidelity to landscape and the necessity for aesthetic transfer have been, for a long time, the subjects of critical controversies. We must note that the processes and movements of de-colonization have succeeded in provoking literary responses, which interpret orature in terms of a medium through which the African writer may re-enter the essence of his culture to draw inspiration. Sometimes this position is stretched to its passionate limit, in which case it presents an approach that tends to prescribe an aesthetic principle for the production of Black literature and its criticism. Boniface Obichere reflects the signature of this canon in offering that orature

> is the incontestable reservoir of the values, sensibilities, aesthetics and achievements of traditional African thought and imagination ... It must serve as the ultimate foundation, guide-post, and point of departure for a modern liberated

---

[5] S. Macebuh, "African Aesthetics in Traditional African Art". *Okike*, 5 (1974): 22.
[6] Mazisi Kunene, "The Relevance of African Cosmological Systems to African Literature Today". *African Literature Today*. 11 (1980): 200.
[7] William Bascom, "Four Functions of Folklore". *Journal of American Folklore*, 67, 226 (1954): 345.
[8] A.H. Gayton, "Perspectives in Folklore". *Journal of American Folklore*, 64, (1951): 149.
[9] O. F. Raum, *Chaga Childhood: A Description of Indigenous Education in an East African Tribe*. (London: OUP, 1940): 214.

African literature. It is the root from which modern liberated African literature must draw its sustenance.[10]

In a book that focuses on understanding the African writing Lamuel Johnson, Bernadette Cailer, Russell Hamilton and Mildred Hill-Lubin re-examine the vexed question of what constitutes the African aesthetic. In this, they rely, quite appropriately, on the platform of the 1980 African Literature Association conference that focused on the central theme of defining the African aesthetic. They put the conclusions of the main paper into three approaches:

> The essays of "tradition and continuity" orientation implicitly offer criteria for the aesthetic by appeals to or illustrations from African oral traditions. The approach makes it clear that those appeals are meant to imply an originally homeophothic, holistic aesthetic ... The assumption here seems to be that the audience or readership is familiar with whatever cognitive, prescriptive and compositional criteria inspire and sustain the "tradition" whose "continuity" is discerned, or negated in the modern texts ... A second approach defines the aesthetic by another strategy. This approach involves an examination or assessment of the degree to which translations, cultural transfers, and the mediations that come with publication affect texts in which "tradition and continuity have achieved a certain compositional and thematic equilibrium ... A third and final approach is through a mediation upon the tools necessary to reach the aesthetic.[11]

The approaches outlined here capture the various transformations and complexities that are encountered in trying to trace the traffic of an African aesthetic existing both as oral and written forms. The current expansion of an 'artist-collective' at the frontiers of aesthetic transfer from tradition has a tendency to create a significant literary movement capable of drawing artists to itself and dictating its own critical approach. The tradition in formation, that is, the on-going process of re-inventing the traditional modes of aesthetic expression in the written medium most accurately indicates a direction in resolving some of the ambiguities provoked by the term 'African aesthetic'.

Still in the book by Johnson *et al*, Kofi Anyidoho joins issues with Richard Dorson on the criteria for determining and authenticating a text's relation with oral traditions. Anyidoho summarizes Dorson's three tests for validating oral art in a written text:

> Richard M. Dorson suggests three tests for establishing the relationship of a given written work to oral tradition: biographical evidence that the author has enjoyed direct contact with oral lore; internal evidence indicating the author's

---

[10] Boniface Obichere (ed.), (Introduction) *Journal of African Studies* 12. 2 (1985): 52.

[11] Lamuel Johnson, *et al* (ed.), *Toward Defining the African Aesthetic*. (Washington DC: Three Continents Press, 1982): 2.

familiarity with folklore; corroborative evidence "that the saying, tale, song, or custom inside the literary work possesses an independent traditional life".[12]

Dorson's third test cannot possibly endure. Oral influences often come as imaginative transfers but not mere replications of forms. As Anyidoho explains,

> Perhaps we do not have to hunt for evidence of folklore as borrowed items only. We may not find a traditional Ewe proverb or fragments of songs in every Awoonor poem or novel, but can we discount the evidence of traditional Ewe styles and techniques of poetic composition? It seems that a writer's ability to adopt and adapt oral styles and techniques is a far more significant case of creative continuity than the incorporation of fragments of folklore into written literature. After all, the good writer is an artist, a creator, not a mere dealer in borrowed items.[13]

As statements from writers who relate with oral traditions creatively indicate, Dorson's second test is more or less subsumed in the first. For instance, Tanure Ojaide, the Nigerian poet comments that

> You have writers who are indebted to the oral traditions because they grew up in that tradition. Most grew up in the rural environment and again, most of them have conducted researches on the oral traditions. Kofi Anyidoho studied African folklore, Niyi Osundare has an oral literature background and for a long time, I have been working on Urhobo *udje* dance songs. So when you are familiar with these forms you are bound to make use of them one way or the other.[14]

Okello Oculli, the Ugandan poet links cultural transfer in artistic works to the authors' real experience with tradition and its multiple aesthetic forms:

> If you are a herd's boy, as you are looking after cattle, you will hear women singing, women who are farming, who are collecting firewood ... thrashing millet, pounding... they will be singing. This cannot but be part of your consciousness. There are cultures with the art of joking where teams are organized on a competitive basis to entertain the audience. Of course if you have not experienced this, if you were locked in a boarding school for instance, and you were never part of the tradition, you will be at a disadvantage. If you have come into contact with this tradition of course you will be influenced by it. If as a child you have experienced religious rituals with chants, invocation of the spirit and so on, this will definitely impact on you. And if you are writing with all the skills that have come into your socialization, it will come in.[15]

---

[12]Kofi Anyidoho, "Kofi Awoonor and the Ewe Tradition of songs of Abuse" in Lamuel Johnson, *et al* (eds.), *Toward Defining the African Aesthetic*. (Washington DC: Three Continents Press, 1982): 17.

[13]ibid.

[14]Charles Bodunde. "Interview with Tanure Ojaide" *Tape Recording* 12th March, 1999 Fez, Morocco.

[15]Charles Bodunde, "Interview with Okello Oculi" *Tape Recording* 13th March 1999 Fez, Morocco.

The pattern of oral transfer varies according to individual artists. For instance, poets like Niyi Osundare and Jack Mapanje employ as many forms as possible to achieve the desired effects in their works. With these poets, one finds, within the space of a single text, varieties such as songs, proverbs, myths and folktales. These oral materials occur in the text as reconstructed forms adapted to new social situations but the essence of their orality (rhythm and performance features) still survive. For some poets, the interest is in a single oral corpus and they seize on the dominant appeal of the genre to explore social and political phenomena. Soyinka, for instance, makes the Ogun myth the core of his art. From this mythic framework, he provokes an engaging dialectic that Femi Osofisan describes as "the double potential of creativity and destruction";[16] the paradox of a deity who is "the god of artists and warriors; both the killer and the poet."[17] In Soyinka's *Idanre*,[18] what we are expected to deal with is the image of Ogun, the god who is described repeatedly as "the iron one", an epithet which expresses the god's violent fury and his creative link with the forge. Christopher Okigbo and Okot p' Bitek are studied for their reflection of the oral voice in form of proverbs, local myths and symbols.

Okinba Launko (Femi Osofisan) explores the Ifa myth as means of social mediation. Launko's treatment of this mythic phenomenon and Kofi Anyidoho's employment of the funeral dirge are examples of the influences of specific oral genres on contemporary Black poetry. Some of the influences in this category are Ojaide's use of *udje*, the Urhobo satirical song and Ezenwa Ohaeto's transfer of the masquerade chant into the space of *The Voice of the Night Masquerade*.

For obvious reasons, African landscape and aesthetic appear to be a matter of great concern to Black writers in the diaspora in spite of the argument advanced by some critics that Black culturalism may turn to mere reaction. The reference point in this regard is Trevor Munroe who states that

> ... because of the extremeness of the psychological oppression of this kind of society one is getting an equally antithetical reaction, and this reaction finds its expression [in] what I call Black culturalism. This means quite simply that people who have become in recent times conscious of the extent to which the society through violent means has whitened them, are now beginning through equally

---

[16]Femi Osofisan, "Soyinka in the Forest of a Thousand Revelers" in Yemi Ogunbiyi (ed.), *Perspectives on Nigerian Literature*. (Lagos: Guardian Books Ltd., 1988): 188.
[17]ibid.
[18]Wole Soyinka, *Idanre and Other Poems*. (London: Methuen, 1967).

extreme measures to re-Africanize themselves, to discover a culture from which they were torn violently.[19]

Kamau Brathwaite's response to this helps to define the essence of Black culturalism in the Caribbean. For him, contrary to being a reaction or divisive, Black culturalism provides "a sense of style and spiritual value - an aesthetic."[20]

Beryl Gilroy describes the kind of imagination that underlines aesthetic transfer within the diaspora context. For this Caribbean writer, the particular interest in oral culture is "the folk stories interspersed with saucy life stories".[21] Gilroy goes further to justify the significance of oral traditions in Caribbean writing:

> Far from being obscurantist, the oral tradition makes Caribbean writing less intrusive, more peaceable and informal. We aim for clarity; its pursuit is a great challenge. We must be able to select from the shadow pool of ideas and images that serve us, and eliminate those which recur as they travel 'by foot and voice'... The written tradition demands studied inventiveness and rigidly fixed elements that conjoin sense and non-sense.[22]

In Caribbean writing, Brathwaite's *The Arrivants* is one of the most successful explorations into oral aesthetics, African history and landscape. Here, the written text reveals the oral mode of performance poetry from which it is created. This is important because such structures lend the text to a performance mode. This kind of transfer is viewed by Ojaide as a normal process in the traffic from orature to the written tradition:

> The inherited performance quality of oral poetry has bearing on the aesthetic composition of modern African poetry ... In other words, verbal composition and performance are intricately related. Since the modern poet is more likely to perform his/her own poetry, these performance qualities are built into the poem. The story told in a poem engenders its own dramatics.[23]

This study examines the various ways in which oral forms are deployed in contemporary Black poetry (in English) to bear cultural and social vision. There is also a concern with the nature of the creativity, which emerges from the poets' relation of borrowed oral forms to contemporary subjects. This obviously implies a determination of the processes involved in sustaining the communicativeness of orature in the written medium thereby making the poems

---

[19]Cited in Edward Kamau Brathwaite, "The Love Axe (1): Developing a Caribbean Aesthetic 1962-1974." *African Studies and Research Center Monograph Series*. 4, (1996): 23.
[20]ibid.
[21]Beryl Gilroy, "The Oral Culture - Effects and Expression". *Wasafiri* 22 (Autumn, 1995): 64.
[22]ibid.
[23]Tanure Ojaide, *Poetic Imagination in Black Africa: Essays on African Poetry*. (Durham: Carolina Academic Press, 1996): 24 -25.

reach out beyond the limitation of its writteness to speak as the oral text does to the audience. The intention is also to point out the various levels of relations or links among the poets to be discussed. These poets are Christopher Okigbo, Okot p' Bitek, Wole Soyinka, Mazisi Kunene, Femi Osofisan, Niyi Osundare, Kofi Anyidoho. Others are Jack Mapanje, Okello Oculi, Obiora Udechukwu, Tanure Ojaide and Ezenwa Ohaeto. Kamau Brathwaite's trilogy, *Rights of Passage*, *Islands* and *Masks* are studied to reflect the nature of cultural transfer and social vision in the aesthetic of the Caribbean poets of the African diaspora.

I. TRADITIONAL POETIC FORMS: THE POETRY OF OKOT P'BITEK AND CHRISTOPHER OKIGBO

Both Okot p'Bitek and Christopher Okigbo are significantly influenced by the oral traditions of their respective cultures. In a significant way, their voices represent early attempts at reconstructing modern Black poetry from the context of oral production. They transfer elements from oral aesthetics to create poetic idioms, which show new vision and remarkable originality. These borrowings occur in the form of imaginative use of local symbols, images, proverbs, myths and other oral aesthetic devices.

Okot p'Bitek's *Song of Lawino*: Symbols

Adrian Roscoe's comment on *Song of Lawino* in his *Uhuru's Fire* touches on Okot p'Bitek's imaginative use of oral traditions. Roscoe argues that Okot p'Bitek's song "has been a truly seminal development" and that its success "stems in part from its relationship to oral tradition".[1] He emphasizes that Okot p'Bitek's achievement is that "better than most African poets, he has created in *Song of Lawino* a form which is popular and the outgrowth of home tradition."[2] Traditional symbols are widely used as techniques in p'Bitek's poetry. Lawino, the speaker of the poem relies on the traditional Acholi symbols of the horn, the bull and the spear to lament her husband's loss of traditional touch.

George Heron's introduction to Heinemann's edition of *Song of Lawino* and *Song of Ocol* helps to establish the key patterns of symbols and tradition among the Acholi. In this culture, the horn for instance, is not only a musical instrument but also a ritual object connected with the whole process of initiation into adulthood. In ceremonies, young men and women normally blow their horns as symbol of their own attributes and reputation. Thus, Lawino speaks of her own fame that spread far beyond her immediate environment like the sound of the horn:

> I was the leader of the girls
> And my name blew like a horn

---

[1] Adrian Roscoe, *Uhuru's Fire*. (London: Cambridge University Press, 1977): 56.
[2] ibid.

> Among the Payira and I played
> On the bow harp and praised my love.³

In her comments on modern day elections, Lawino also uses the horn symbol for effect. She talks of the "horn loud and proud" of the victorious in contrast to the silent horn of the defeated.

Also among the Acholi, the bull is a panegyric title used as a compliment for bravery and respect. Lawino combines the symbols of the bull and the horn to remind Ocol, her husband, of the respectable and famous ancestry from which he descends. She indicts Ocol for behaving like "a dog of the white man" (p. 116) and reminds him of his proud ancestry:

> Your grandfather was a Bull among men
> And although he died long ago
> His name still blows like a horn
> His name is still heard
> Throughout the land (p. 116)

Like the horn, the spear possesses a ritual essence. Among the Acholi, it is part of the tradition to bury the dead with his spear placed by his side. The phallic significance of the spear is obvious. It is a symbol of masculinity and Lawino employs it to capture Ocol's alienation and impotence and the need for him to recover his tradition and manhood:

> When you have gained your full strength
> Go to the shrine of your father,
> Prepare a feast ...
> Beg forgiveness from them
> And ask them to give you a new spear
> A new spear with a sharp and hard point
> A spear that will crack the rock
> Ask for a spear that you will thrust...
> Ask them to restore your manhood!
> For I am sick of sharing a bed with a woman (p. 119)

With the spear symbol, p'Bitek makes a major statement concerning the effects of modernization. In this, Ocol is used to illustrate the prodigal complex or the outcast syndrome which modernity helps to create.

---

³ Okot p'Bitek, *Song of Lawino* and *Song of Ocol*. (London: Heinemann, 1984): 48. All subsequent page references are made to this edition and appear in the text.

Images, Proverbs and Myths

Heron makes an important statement that underscores the uniqueness of p'Bitek's use of traditional imagery:

> The most important influence Acholi songs have on *Song of Lawino* is the imagery Okot uses. Okot has completely avoided the stock of common images of English literature through his familiarity with the stock of common images of Acholi literature. (p. 7)

Heron stresses that in the English version, the stock of Acholi imagery "gives his poem a feeling of freshness for every reader, and a sense of Africaness for African readers". (p. 7)

Lawino engages traditional images to criticize Clementina, her rival over Ocol. She describes the woman's lips as "red-hot like glowing charcoal" (p. 37) and when she "dusts powder on her face, she resembles the wizard getting ready for the midnight dance" (p. 37). This image appropriately captures the weird adornment that shows on Clementina's face.

Section eleven of the book presents Independence in the image of a fallen buffalo which the eager politicians, rush to share like hunters:

> Independence falls like a bull buffalo
> And the hunters rush to it with drawn knives
> Sharp shining knives for carving the carcass
> And if your chest is small, bony and weak
> They push you off, and if your knife is blunt
> You get the dung on your elbow,
> You come home empty handed
> And the dogs bark at you! (p. 107)

In the same section of the poem, Lawino exposes the poverty and neglect, which the voters are forced to bear after each election. The politicians "who have fallen into things", throw themselves "into soft beds while the hip bones of the voters grow painful, sleeping on the same earth they slept before Uhuru!" (p. 110). She castigates politicians who abandon the voters and are rarely seen again after their election victory. Like the python "with a bull water buck in its tummy" (p. 110), the politicians "hibernate and stay away and eat" (p. 110). Lawino takes the image of the kite from the Acholi song and adapts it to convey the exploitative attitude of the modern day African politicians who "return to the countryside for the next election/like the kite/That returns during the Dry Season" (p. 110).

Proverbs are common features of the oral tradition. In *Songs of Lawino*, the central proverb is the one built on the pumpkin. In the Acholi oral tradition, the pumpkin planted around the homestead is never uprooted even when the old homestead is to be abandoned. The proverb, "The pumpkin in the old homestead/must not be uprooted" recurs in the poem. Lawino uses this proverb to warn Ocol who has not only embraced the new way of life brought by modernization but is set to destroy his old origin, represented as "the pumpkin in the old homestead". Apart from proverbs, p'Bitek uses traditional sayings to enhance his vision of the Black world. When Lawino points to the need for an African to be himself, she reveals her vision through a witty local saying constructed around animal figures:

> No leopard
> would change into a hyena
> And the crested crane
> would hate to be changed
> Into the bald-headed
> Dung eating vulture
> The long-necked and graceful giraffe
> Cannot become a monkey. (p. 56)

One of the technical devices used by p'Bitek in *Song of Lawino* is the incorporation of the Acholi myth to shape Lawino's character as well as to locate the setting of the poem. Unable to relate to the process by which electricity works, Lawino falls back to the myth surrounding this in her tradition:

> They say
> When the Rain-cock
> Opens its wings
> The blinding light
> And the deadly fire
> Flow through the wires
> And lighten the streets
> And the houses
> And the fire
> Goes into the electric stove. (p. 57)

By making Lawino to speak this way, p'Bitek sets her apart from Ocol, who is evidently lost to Lawino's simple world. Although Ocol may laugh at Lawino's ignorance, his uprooted status is far more pathetic.

Repetition and Audience Involvement

In *Songs of Lawino,* phrases are repeated as in the oral performance. The repetition of "Let no one uproot the pumpkin" throughout the sections of the book is intended to emphasize Lawino's attempt to preserve traditional values in

11

the face of the destructive influence of Western tradition. Ocol receives verbal lashings from Lawino for alienating himself from his own roots. In a biting criticism of the relationship between Ocol and Clementina, Lawino repeats the line "As white people do" in a song-like rendering to emphasize Ocol's obsession with the white man's social values:

> You kiss her on the cheek
> As white people do.
> You kiss her open sore lips
> As white people do
> You suck the slimy saliva
> From each other's mouths
> As white people do. (p. 44)

Audience involvement is a significant aspect of the oral art. Abu Abarry states that this is so important that its removal will render any oral performance meaningless.[4] Lawino's eagerness to involve the audience in her narration is indicated in the song-like type of repetition illustrated above and a direct address to the audience signaled by expressions like "come brother" and "my clansman". These devices provide insight into the nature of oral aesthetic, which one may describe generally as a collective production involving the oral performer and the audience.

Christopher Okigbo's *Path of Thunder*: Symbols and Images

Although Okigbo is greatly indebted to European poets, there is sufficient evidence of traditional materials in his poetry. Even the "Troika", Chinweizu, Jemie and Madubuike, who criticize him along with other poets for what they call "obscurantism and senseless narcissism" in his earlier poems, nevertheless appreciate the function of the oral traditions in *Path of Thunder*:

> The high peak attained by Okigbo in "Path of Thunder" towers above the low irregular landscape of Nigerian poetry in English. So far, the only other peak that rivals it in African poetry in English is Okot p'Bitek's *Song of Lawino* which is possibly the best rounded single work of African poetry in English today.[5]

---

[4] Abu Abarry, "Oral Rhetoric and Poetics", S.O. Asein (ed.), *Comparative Approaches to Modern African Literature*. (Ibadan: Dept. of English, University of Ibadan, 1984): 24.

[5] Chinweizu *et al*, *Toward the Decolonization of African Literature*. (Enugu: Fourth Dimension, 1980): 187.

[6] Christopher Okigbo, *Labyrinths*. (London: Heinemann, 1971). All page references are made to this edition and appear in the text.

The ritual and sacrificial ceremonies in "Lustra" are heightened through skillful association of images and symbols. In this section of *Labyrinths*,[6] the poet, who has been alienated from his indigenous culture, now comes back like a prodigal wishing to be readmitted into communion with the goddess, Idoto. Dan Izevbaye emphasizes the significance of the ritual offering on the part of the prodigal-poet. He notes that since the poet is technically a stranger, he requires ritual cleansing. The three parts of "Lustra" are therefore concerned with this traditional feast of purification. The "traditionally prescribed objects of purification" like vegetable offerings, chalk, long-drums and cannons are ritual symbols that show the poet's struggle for acceptance.[7] In the rest of *Labyrinths*, images and symbols such as "palm-grove", "weaver-bird", "the town crier", "the hornbill" and "the sacrificial ram", are used to capture the exploration of the poet-persona in his search for poetic illumination, purification, acceptance and integration into his traditional culture.

Traditional Poetic Forms

Okigbo borrows the invocational and incantatory devices from the oral traditions and uses them imaginatively to draw attention to the traditional religion from which he has been exiled and to which he now returns like a prodigal. In *Labyrinths,* the scenes of sacrifices are occasions for incantations and invocation. This indigenous influence is noted by Romanus Egudu who affirms that Okigbo's adaptation of the tone of incantation for the ritual scenes is consistent with the use in which this traditional form is put "by every Igbo high priest of the indigenous god."[8]

Sometimes, Okigbo makes an innovative combination of the techniques of invocation, incantation and the traditional praise poetry. For instance, in "Siren Limits", he invokes the goddess of the palm groves reflecting the structure of the praise tradition:

> Queen of the damp half-light,
> I have had my cleansing.
> Emigrant with air-borne nose,
> The he-goat-on-heat. (p. 23)

---

[7] Dan Izevbaye, "Okigbo's Portrait of the Artist as a Sunbird: A Reading of *Heavensgate*". *African Literature Today*, 6 (1973): 20.

[8] Romanus Egudu, "Defense of Culture in the Poetry of Christopher Okigbo". *African Literature Today*, 6 (1973): 10.

The traditional praise poem influences a segment of Okigbo's "Hurrah for Thunder". In the second stanza of this poem, he describes the might of the elephant (which may be taken to represent the power of the ruling class) in a praise chant:

> The elephant, tetrarch of the jungle:
> With a wave of the hand
> He could pull four trees to the ground;
> His four mortar legs pounded the earth:
> Wherever they treaded,
> The grass was forbidden to be there. (p. 67)

The description of the attributes of the elephant echoes the traditional chants (especially the Yoruba *Ijala*) on this animal by the oral artist. S.A. Babalola for instance argues that verbal salute to particular animals is one of the dominant subjects of the *Ijala* praise poetry. He stresses that the oral artist does this by giving

> a character sketch of the said animal or bird. Such a chant contains information about the physical appearance, the characteristic gait and the characteristic habits of the animal or bird.[9]

Some of the animals identified as subjects of this oral genre are the elephant, the buffalo, the lion and the baboon. Okigbo's "Hurrah for Thunder" is an imaginative transfer of this kind of poetry into a written form. The imaginative use of the praise form allows for an equally imaginative political interpretation. The elephant becomes a symbol of the powerful political force which threatened to destroy the four regions of Nigeria in the sixties (the "four mortar legs") "with a wave of the hand". This brute force is further underscored in the image of an elephant pulling "four trees to the ground."

Proverbs, Repetitions and Musical Accompaniments

Okigbo's *Labyrinths* contains proverbs that are borrowed from oral traditions and modified to suit the socio-political vision intended in the poetry. Helen Chukwuma stresses the usefulness of proverbs and the ways in which they could be borrowed and modified to project certain opinions:

> Proverbs are used to express an essential idea. When they are used in verse, they are not usually subject to a rendition in their original forms. Rather they are modified and adapted according to the demand of rhythm and beat. Adaptation

---

[9] S.A. Babalola, *The Content and Form of Yoruba Ijala*. (London: Oxford University Press, 1966): 11.

may take the form of adding a few words or of contrasting the proverb words while still retaining the essential image necessary for its identification.[10]

Again in "Hurrah for Thunder", Okigbo hears the hunters, the military, "already ... talking about pumpkins" (p. 67). The poet's duty is also to warn the society and in doing this, Okigbo uses the proverb technique to bear the weight of his warning: "The eye that looks down will surely see the nose" and "The finger that fits should be used to pick the nose" (p. 67). The two proverbs are direct translations from the local stock of proverbs. The first one is strikingly close to the type used by Agboreko in Wole Soyinka's *A Dance in the Forests*:

> OLD MAN: Yes, yes, we'll be patient.
> AGBOREKO: The eye that looks downwards will certainly see the nose.[11]

What Okigbo wants to communicate through this proverb is similar to Agboreko's amplification of Old Man's plea for patience. Okigbo uses the proverb to caution those who hold political power to exercise patience and wisdom especially at the crucial moment of crisis.

Like p'Bitek, Okigbo uses repetition as a rhetorical device. Chukwuma describes this device as "a basic principle of oral art and can be viewed as a stylistic and fundamental grammatical form". She argues that, "verbal repetition in oral art is sometimes used as a way of establishing emphasis" and that "in a typical oral verse, repetition entails not only the structure but the words of the stanzas themselves."[12] The device of repetition contributes immensely to the musical quality of Okigbo poetry. In "Elegy for Slit-drum" where the traditional dirge form is used, repetition helps to intensify the aura of grief as well as the sense of instability that befalls the nation. The word "condolences" is repeated several times in this section of the poem. Also, some lines are repeated to evoke the elevated sound effect suitable for the dirge form. The following lines illustrate these functions:

> the panther has delivered a hare
> the hare is beginning to leap
> the panther has delivered a hare
> the panther is about to leap. (p. 68)

And:

> the elephant has fallen
> the mortars have won the day

---

[10] Helen Chukwuma, "The Oral Nature of Traditional Poetry and Language". *Journal of the Nigerian English Studies,* 8, 1 (May 1976): 17.

[11] Wole Soyinka, *A Dance in the Forests*. (Oxford: Oxford University Press, 1963): 38.

[12] Helen Chukwuma: 16.

> the elephant has fallen
> does he deserve his fate
> the elephant has fallen
> can we remember the date. (p. 67)

Okigbo also uses parallelism as a form of repetition. This type creates a certain kind of melody and it also intensifies the emotional impact that the poet intends to register. An example of this form of repetition is the couplet that ends "Elegy for Slit-drum":

> trunk of the iron tree we cry *condolences* when we break.
> shells of the open sea we cry *condolences* when we shake (p. 70)

And in "Distances VI", we have yet another:

> I have fed out of the drum
> I have drunk out of the cymbal (p. 60)

Ulli Beier, who is renowned for his work among oral artists in Nigeria and elsewhere gives a description of the musical quality of Okigbo's poetry:

> Everything he touches vibrates and swings and we are compelled to read on and to follow the tune of his chant, hardly worried about the fact that we understand little of what he has to say.[13]

Okigbo uses drum and rattles accompaniments in "Elegy for Alto" and "Elegy for Slit-drum" to create a sense of national mourning. This is consistent with the use of musical instruments like flute, resonated pot and rattles in oral production where poetry is rendered in the ambience of other art forms. There is no doubt that Okigbo shows his originality in the fashioning of new poetic idioms from oral aesthetic resources. Okigbo's intensely resonant poetry is celebrated by many of the poets who lament his death in *Don't Let Him Die*.[14]

Although the modern African poet does not see himself using exactly the same method as the oral artist as Echeruo observes,[15] the echoes of traditional symbols, images and idioms create a distinctive aesthetic form that resonate the artistic experience and vision of the Black world. This is the glowing legacy which both writers left for other African poets.

---

[13] Ulli Beier, "Reactions to 'Siren Limits' ". *Black Orpheus*, 12 (1963): 46-47.

[14] Chinua Achebe and Dubem Okafor (eds.), *Don't Let Him Die*. (Enugu: Fourth Dimension Publishers, 1978.)

[15] M.J. Echeruo, "Traditional and Borrowed Elements in Nigerian Poetry". *Nigerian Magazine*, 89 (June 1966): 142.

II. MYTH, LEGEND AND THE POETICS OF HEROISM

With a number of African poets, an interesting pattern emerges from an aesthetic apprehension of certain African myths and legends. There is a remarkable demonstration of the connectedness between myth and legend in the ways in which Soyinka relates Ogun with Shaka and also the ways in which Soyinka's image of Ogun connects Kunene's vision of Shaka as a revolutionary archetype. The works of Soyinka, Kunene and Senghor are essential in tracing these levels of connection.

The Ogun image in Soyinka's *Idanre*

Jeyifo's observation on Soyinka's Ogun is a useful summary of the various sections of *Idanre*:

> Ogun is at once a creator and destroyer, at once gregarious, extroverted and reclusive, at once a hunter and warrior (a man of action) and a mystic (a man of thought). Soyinka has also divined a scientific temper in his chosen deity.[1]

Lois Adams emphasizes the more positive side of Ogun in arguing that the god is associated with the earth (as a source of iron ore) and the ritual celebrations connected with the fertility of the earth.[2] Adeboye Babalola simply describes Ogun as "the Yoruba god of war and iron implements"[3] while Isidore Okpewho sees Ogun as "the god of blood and iron, of war and the deadly hunt."[4] Wande Abimbola's image of Ogun is particularly relevant. For him, Ogun is the iron divinity charged with exploiting his extra-ordinary physical power to tackle all problems of warfare and heroism.[5] In a significant way, Afam Ebeogu's description of Ogun as "the ubiquitous god, who destroys as he creates"[6] captures the essential thrust of this myth. This interplay of the creative and the destructive is most evident in Soyinka's *Idanre*.

---

[1] Biodun Jeyifo, "What is the will of Ogun?" in Yemi Ogunbiyi (ed.), *Perspective on Nigerian Literature* (Lagos: Guardian Books Ltd., 1988): 175.

[2] Lois Adams, *The Prison and Post-prison Writing of Wole Soyinka*. (PhD dissertation, University of Wisconsin, Madison, 1980): xix.

[3] Adeboye Babalola, "The Traditional Poetry of Yoruba Hunters" in Ulli Beier (ed.), *Introduction to African Literature* (London: Longman, 1979): 12.

[4] Isidore Okpewho, *The Epic in Africa*. (New York: Columbia University Press, 1979): 47.

[5] Wande Abimbola, *Sixteen Great Poems of Ifa*. (New York: UNESCO, 1975): 3.

[6] Afam Ebeogu, "From *Idanre* to *Ogun Abibiman*: An Examination of Soyinka's Use of Ogun Image". *Journal of Commonwealth Literature*, 15, 1 (August 1980): 86.

Idanre opens with the unsettling chaos of inchoate earth in the process of creation. The two gods (Ogun and Sango) are associated with this force and the battle between them reflects the general atmosphere of chaos. The gods battle each other with weapons that we now recognize as the symbols of their power. Ogun's fiery physical power is summoned in combat against Sango's "way-ward bolts."[7] Ogun plucks the last ember of Sango's fire, which has laced the cosmic space with fire tracings and then battles the fire god to earth:

> He catches Sango in his three-fingered
> hand
> And runs him down to earth. Safe
> shields my eaves
> This night, I have set the Iron One
> against
> All wayward bolts. (p. 61)

The primeval battle,[8] accompanied with fire and rain in complex fusion gives earth its organic matter:

> And no one speaks of secrets in
> this land
> Only, that the skin be bared
> to welcome rain
> And earth prepare, that seeds
> may swell
> And roots take flesh within her,
> and men
> Wake naked into harvest-tide. (p. 61)

Thus, this opening section introduces Ogun as a god whose being radiates abundant physical energy. This is Ogun's strongest virtue. He is only able to subdue Sango by exploiting his store of energy. This gift of energy becomes Ogun's greatest support in his battles. Soyinka refers to Ogun's physical strength in the recurrent epithet of "the iron one". The poet's description of the god's descent into Earth reveals the source of this power. Ogun, we are told, has armed himself with the first technical weapon which "he has forged from the ore

---

[7] Wole Soyinka, *Idanre and Other Poems*. (London: Methuen, 1969): 61. All subsequent page references are made to this edition and appear in the text.

[8] See Wole Soyinka, *Myth Literature and the African World*. (London: Cambridge University Press, 1978): 151. Here, Soyinka interprets Ogun's battle with Sango as the primal combat of the gods. Ogun invests his energy and will to claim victory.

of mountain-wombs"⁹ and has "cleared the primordial jungle, plunged through the abyss and called on the others to follow."¹⁰

Ogun's dual essences of creativity and destruction also reflect in the blood icon, which as Soyinka uses it, embodies sacrifice and recreation. In this respect, the slaughter of the wine girl is symbolic. In a curious shift of action, Ogun smiles at the girl and then kills her, spilling her blood on the road:

> The sky cracked halfway,
> a greying skull
> on blooded highways. I turned,
> vapors rose
> From sodden bitumen and snaked within
> Her wrap of indigo, her naval
> misted over
> a sloe bared from the fruit. (p. 63)

With this blood sacrifice, Ogun walks "across a haze of corn" (p. 63) teasing his ears with tassels. Furthermore, the road that "waits, famished" (p. 64) is the trap for blood sacrifice. The wheels on the road are equally the metaphor for the traffic of death. Here again, Soyinka details destruction and recreation in a complex fusion of the images of growth and death. We hear of "Fated lives" (p. 64) that "ride on the wheels of death" (p. 64), the "errant wheel/of the death chariot" (p. 65) and "rich blood spilt, brain and marrow making manure" with "sheep excrement" (p. 65) to stimulate the growth in plants.

In section III, titled "Pilgrimage", the poet sets on another journey to Idanre. Adventurous like his muse, the poet links past memory of Idanre hills with new voyage:

> This road have I trodden in a time beyond
> Memory of fallen leaves, beyond
> Thread of fossil on the slate, yet
> I must
> This way again. (p. 69)

In this section, the poet describes the elemental fury that accompanies Ogun, the iron god. In a violent motion across Idanre hills, Ogun creates sparks that illuminate his paths. The poet tells us, Ogun's knees "struck sparks to brim the night/brushing rocks in self-rage up the hill" (p. 70). Ogun's habitat is the belly of rock shields, a place lit with the flames of active volcano:

> Low beneath rock shields, home

---

⁹ ibid:29.
¹⁰ ibid.

> of the iron One
> The sun had built a fire within
> Earth's hearthstone. Flames in fever fits
> Rain in rock fissures, and hill surfaces
> Were all aglow with earth's
> transparency. (p. 70)

The fire symbol re-echoes Ogun's creative essence especially when this is viewed in relation to the link that Soyinka makes between Ogun and Sango, the fire god. Ogun rises against the "plague of finite chaos" (p. 70) to clear the path for man. Ogun, the artisan god ("primal mechanic" p. 71) creates his weapon of war from Sango's spent thunderbolt.

Ogun creates in fury and there is a sort of willful violence in his intervention. The god encounters the human society "with his leather war-kit, smeared in blood from head to foot."[11] However, this symbolic demonstration of blood is lost on the Ire elders who persuade him to be their king. Unknown to them, they have crowned the god "who bathes in rivers of Blood."[12] They have brought an angry god to supper without "a long bamboo pole" (p. 72) and have "hired a hunter, filled him with wine/and thrust a fire brand in his hand." (p. 72) In battle, Ogun, already drunk, rises to the occasion of war with tremendous physical energy destroying his own men:

> Tall he rises to the hills
> His head a rain-cloud has eclipsed the sun
> His nostrils blow visible
> Exhalations as twin-flues through clouds
> There are myriad lesser motes in flight
> And leaping mists. Never to his ears,
> Never to him comes the cry of men
> In sweet lather of death.
> > Lord of all witches, divine hunter
> > Your men Ogun, your men! (p. 74)

But Ogun is deaf to the people's protest and still,

> He strides sweet encrusted
> Bristles on risen tendons
> Porcupine and barbed. Again, he turns
> Into his men, a butcher's axe
> Rises and sinks. (p. 75)

---

[11] Wole Soyinka, *Myth, Literature and the African World*, 29.
[12] ibid:26.

In their tragic discovery the people moan that they have summoned a god who inhabits the domain of chaos:

> Where do we seek him, they asked?
> Where conflict rages, where sweat
> Is torrent of rain, where clear springs
> Of blood fill one with longing
> As the rush of wine. (p. 75)

Thus, the images of fire, blood and chaos depict Ogun as man's inventive will and also that violence which normally accompanies such will.

The Image of Shaka

Shaka, the well-known king of the Zulu in the early part of the 19th century is, in literature, an enigmatic figure. William Worger's description of him as "dry bones clad in contestable historiographic clothing"[13] is an appropriate metaphor for the apparent conflicting historical depictions of this character. The same idea is expressed by John Kesby who argues that although Shaka is "as well authenticated as his contemporary, Napoleon, the tradition about him which were current after his death (in 1828) are probably unreliable and certainly do not agree with each other."[14] C. F. J. Muller portrays Shaka as a warrior and tactician without equal. He however quarrels with his ruthless expansionist pursuit.[15] C. T. Binns who praises Shaka for his genius in building up the mightiest fighting force that Africa had ever known condemns his cruel methods of execution.[16] To some historians, Shaka was simply a tyrant with an untamable lust for blood. For instance, Brian Roberts describes Shaka as an irrational king who "had no set objectives and was uninfluenced by political and moral considerations."[17] Freda Troup also argues that Shaka "maintained his position in large part by terror; executions and massacres were common enough events."[18] He emphasizes that the Zulu king "became a cruel, sadistic and widely feared tyrant" who made most of central Natal a land of devastation and

---

[13] William Worger, "Clothing Dry Bones: The Myth of Shaka". *Journal of African Studies* 3, (1989):156.

[14] John D. Kesby, "African Legends" in Richard Cavendish (ed.), *Legends of the World*. (London: Orbits Publishing Ltd., 1982): 319.

[15] C. F. J. Muller, *Five Hundred Years: A History of South Africa*. (Pretoria: H & R Academics, 1971): 497.

[16] C.T. Binns, *The Last Zulu King*. (London: Longmans, Green & Co. Ltd., 1963):176.

[17] Brian Roberts, *The Zulu Kings*. (New York: Charles Scribner & Sons, 1974): 156.

[18] Freda Troup, *South Africa: An Historical Introduction*. (London: Eyre Methuen Ltd., 1972): 40.

desolation by 1824.[19] This kind of portrait is also sustained in Thomas Mofolo's *Chaka*.[20] Mofolo's choice of the historical romance genre allows him to incorporate the most nihilistic traits to create the image of a man who personifies evil. Mofolo's use of fictional characters like Noliwa, Isanusi, Malunga and Ndlebe contributes to this negative portrait.

In a way, the enigma that surrounds Shaka's image provokes a wide range of literary intentions and portraits. In their individual works, Mazisi Kunene, Wole Soyinka and Sedar Senghor make aesthetic interpretations of the Shaka phenomenon and what we finally see is the image of a revolutionary archetype.

Mazisi Kunene and the Shaka Epic

In the epic, *Emperor Shaka the Great*, Kunene celebrates Shaka by giving account of his military skill and vision. The poet invites us into the world of Shaka through the device of direct address in which we hear Shaka, the warlord, giving details of his military strategy. In the various sections of the epic, we hear Shaka's confident voice as he addresses his regiments: "the essence of success in war is speed/speed is of the mind and all intricacies of wars.../speed is of the feet not encumbered by sandals".[21] As a warrior king, Shaka introduces further military ideas to make his army invulnerable. He enforces military drills, which are intended to prepare his army adequately for battle. Shaka discovers that the long spear is too cumbersome, so he invents the short spear that is effective in close combat. Kunene cites the great battle with Zwide as an event in which Shaka demonstrates the most intelligent military strategy. First, he plans a tight spying scheme through Prince Mzilikasi who in turn works through an insider to collect information on Zwide's battle strategy. He later uses a more sophisticated reconnaissance plan against the recalcitrant Faku.

Kunene celebrates other dimensions of Shaka's of image through elaborate allusions to his military vision. The poet builds images around Shaka's argument for absolute war instead of the half-hearted battles under Dingiswayo. He has once argued that, "the enemy must be chased and trapped in his own home" (p. 51) otherwise he will "re-emerge, again and again.../like the menace of weeds in a fertile field..." (p. 51). Early in the epic, Shaka says

---

[19] ibid.

[20] Thomas Mofolo, *Chaka: An Historical Romance*. Trans. by F.H. Dutton (London: Oxford University Press, 1971).

[21] Mazisi Kunene, *Emperor Shaka the Great*. (London: Heinemann, 1979): 54. All subsequent page references are made to this edition and appear in the text.

philosophically, "what fights a war is not numbers, nor weapons, but the mind" (p. 84). He extends this later through an aphorism: "wars are fought not only through numbers/or the cleverness of strategies but also through beliefs" (p. 127).

Kunene's book is a translated oral epic of the Zulu. Evidence of oral composition is therefore reflected in the various elements of heroic poetry and other oral aesthetic genres, which help to develop the actions and setting of the epic. Kunene retains the Zulu praise tradition to give Shaka a superhuman image. For instance, the young praise singer from Izichwe associates Shaka with thunder and lion: "Thunderbolt that fell into the House of Phungashe" (p. 60) and "Multi-voiced one who is like a lion" (p. 60). In the heart of the celebration of the famed heroes of the Khahlamba, the lion image reoccurs in Magolwana's praise chant for Shaka: "He is like a lion that wakes up with the morning/And devours the cattle of the villages." (p. 246)

The heroic poet connects his art with the physical environment around him drawing images and symbols for the purpose of representing the character of the epic hero. Often, the images occur as repeated epithet to emphasize the dominant attribute of the hero. Kunene sustains this form of aesthetic relation especially in creating his own portrait of Shaka. One of the most memorable instances of the relation of art and ecology is the rendition of Shaka's praise poem during the king's visit to Zihlandlo. As Kunene describes it, the local poet chants Shaka's praise from the top of the mist-covered mountain. The poet, conscious of his environment skillfully associates Shaka's physical appearance with animal figures, mountains and a wide variety of plants in the Zulu landscape:

> He, who is as huge as his own vast territories
> He, who is first among all the great Ancestors,
> like the giant mountains of Sondude,
> Under which the Ndwandwes and the Nxumalos sat,
> Like the giant tree that is perched on Maqhwakaza ridge...
> It is as if I am looking at a poisonous euphorbia tree.
> The great crooked rook of Mdlaka:
> He rears high like the ocean
> Which roars and lashes eternally.
> Wild one, who is like the unruly ear of an angry elephant,
> Like a paste of poisonous millet grains...
> You are the dragon! The leopard! The lion!
> You are like an old fierce black mamba! You are the elephant!
> You are as huge as the tall mountains of Mphehlela and
>   Maqhwakazi. (p. 308)

It is traditional for the king to reserve special praise poems for his war generals. In one of the poems of praise given to Shaka by Dingiswayo, the hero is captured in cosmic and animal images:

> 'The slow-climbing sun of Mdlala -
> When it rose the morning stars warned each other.
> One was of Ntombazi; another was of Langa!
> Round calabashes that are bought
> Are beautiful like the sun!
> He came down the mountain
> On which no beast ever descended
> Only the millipedes tumbled down!
> Black one, who is like the rich fields of mud!
> You are as huge as the giant tree at the hilltop
> You are like the young of the buck!
> Pathfinder, who opened the way to Ntumeni and eShowe cities.
> The great bird returned by the landmarks of all trees. (p. 113)

It is interesting to note that the pathfinder archetype employed by the praise chanter in this section of Kunene's epic relates to the path-maker symbol, which we find in Soyinka's works on Ogun mythology. This is of course one of the connections between the Ogun myth and the Shaka legend.

Kunene retains the performance atmosphere of the traditional epic poet by drawing upon the chants of the oral artists who render Shaka's praise poems. For instance, the praise chant immediately after Shaka's death reflects the sound formation and direct address techniques typical of performance poetry: In this chant, the cumulative arrangement of the names of Shaka's victims evokes a powerful rhetorical effect that is most suitable to a final rite of passage to a hero:

> He overwhelmed Matshingele of the Khulumbeni region.
> He captured Gwayi of Mazindela.
> He captured Mpangala of Nomgqobo.
> He overcame Phalaza of Khanyile. (p. 425)

The chanter apostrophizes Shaka in a brilliant shift from the first person reference to the second person mode:

> You brought Mangcengceza of Khali among the Mbathas.
> You humbled Matiwane, the son of Masumpa of the Ngwanes.
> You punished Makhedama of emaLangeni among your mother's people...
> You destroyed Sigawuzana of the stubborn Mbatha clan.
> You, the deep pool that is centred in the river of Mayiwane:
> You captured Mphezeni of the Nxumalos...
> You crossed by the short route the regions of Madlungela. (p. 426)

Senghor and Soyinka on Shaka

As expected, Senghor's image of Shaka is influenced by his Negritude vision. Anna Ridehaigh provides reasons why the Shaka subject is attractive to the Négritude writer:

> Shaka was viewed as a nation-builder, a unifier of his people. From this perspective, he is presented as the forerunner of Négritude and the independence movement. Faced with the encroachment of white traders and the fragmented nature of African societies, he welded a number of these societies together into a unified political force with a strong central government.[22]

For a Négritude writer like Senghor, Shaka personifies the unifying force, which was later eroded by colonial fragmentation. This is the predominant image in Senghor's *Chaka*.

In this dramatic poem, Senghor employs the voice and chorus techniques to present the Shaka story. The two main voices in the poem are those of Shaka and the white man. These two voices are symbolic. Here, Shaka is the African voice speaking against oppression and proclaiming the humanism of "brotherhood with equality".[23] Shaka describes White Voice as "voice of the strong against the weak, conscience of the possessors from across the sea" (p. 148). Senghor's intention here is simple. The poem is a defense of the image of Shaka. In the exchanges between the voices, we hear Shaka denying the killer image, which White Voice imposes on him. He describes himself as a mind opposed to segregation "in the kraal of misery" (p. 147). The Chorus seizes on this and celebrates Shaka as the Muse from whom Africans "draw strong life ... the broad backed who carry all the black-skinned peoples". (p. 152)

Although Soyinka is strongly opposed to Senghor's Negritude, there is however a common pursuit in their aesthetic apprehension of the Shaka story. Soyinka's image of Shaka in *Ogun Abibiman* is that of an astute nation builder whose moral collapse "we can only surmise as manic depression".[24] His vitriol against Shaka's critic is also revealing:

> The professional apologists of our time have tried, uncritically, to place in the same category of leaders as Shaka, that murderous buffon who straddles territory where the great Shaka trod. (p. 23)

---

[22] Anna Ridehalgh, "Some Recent Francophone Versions of the Shaka Story". *Research in African Literatures* 22, 2 (1991): 149.

[23] Quotations from Senghor's *Chaka* are made from John Read and Clive Wake, *Senghor: Prose and Poetry*. (London: Heinemann, 1979): 147.

[24] Wole Soyinka, *Ogun Abibiman*. (London: Rex Collings, 1976): 23. All subsequent page references are made to this edition and appear in the text.

In Soyinka's *Ogun Abibiman*, the mythic and legendary figures are fused. Ogun fraternizes with Shaka. Ogun's energy and will are reincarnated in the legend of Shaka. Ogun's service to the Ire people is also related to Shaka's military pursuit among the Zulu. In Soyinka's portrait, Shaka is eager to build a nation from the sparseness of Nguni land. He envisions a "race which beckoned [to him] from the slaughter valley to the hill of destiny" (p. 12). As Soyinka lashes at those who "pollute the wind/with idiot tales" (p. 16) to defame Shaka, the choric refrain, rendered in Yoruba and the echo of Shaka's praise name celebrate Ogun-Shaka link:

> -Sigidi!
> Sigidi Baba! Bayete!
> Rogbodiyan! Rogbodiyan!
> Ogun re le e Shaka
> Rogbodiyan
> Ogun gbo wo o Shaka
> O di rogbodiyan
>
> (Turmoil on turmoil!
> Ogun treads the earth of Shaka.
> Turmoil on the loose
> Ogun Shakes the hand of Shaka
> All is in turmoil.)[25]

The points of interest in the recast of the myth of Ogun and the legend of Shaka lie in the ways in which the individual poets have been able to connect these oral forms with contemporary social realities. This is reflected in the general tone of nationalism contained in Senghor' and Soyinka's portrait of Shaka. With both Ogun and Shaka, there is the replication of the archetypal hero whose vision and struggle represent new ways of dealing with reality.

---

[25] Soyinka's translation, see Glossary, Wole Soyinka, *Ogun Abibiman*: 24.

III. MYTH AND AESTHETIC MEDIATION: IFA DIVINATION POETRY AND OKINBA LAUNKO'S POETRY

The central idea and form in Okinba Launko's *Dream-Seeker on Divining Chain* derive from Ifa (Yoruba) divination poetry. A study of the ways in which aesthetic transfer works in this text therefore requires a brief explanation of the nature of the Ifa corpus.

Ifa divination is at the centre of the Yoruba tradition and all aspects of this mytho-aesthetic canon are organized to explain the nature of human life and the tending of life itself through a divination system that offers answers to common human problems. Ifa, (also known as Orunmila) is the deity of divination. Existing scholarship on this mythology owes much to the efforts of Wande Abimbola who has made the most comprehensive and illuminative collections of Ifa divination poetry. Abimbola describes Ifa as "the Yoruba god of wisdom, knowledge and divination" who occupies "a premier position among Yoruba divinities."[1] He argues further that Ifa's supreme status is derived from his vast knowledge and wisdom.[2] Abimbola identifies the six iconic objects of Ifa divination as *Ikin* (the sacred sixteen palm nuts), *opele* (the divining chain), *Ibo* (instruments for casting lots). Others are *Iyerosun* (divination powder), *Iroke* (carved wooden or ivory object) and *opon Ifa* (the divining tray)[3]. Of these objects, the divining chain and the divining tray are the two objects most conspicuous to any casual observer of the act of divination. As Abimbola explains, the Ifa priest "uses the divining chain for most of his day-to-day divination involving his numerous clients and reserves the sacred palm nuts for more important occasions." In the divination process, the Ifa priest

> Holds the chain in the middle of its top region and throws it away from himself. When the chain falls to the ground, each of the four half-nuts on either side will present its outside or inside surface upwards. There are 2^8 possibilities of this form of presentation each time the Ifa priest throws his chain. Each of these possibilities of presentation is known as *odù* or chapter in the Ifa divination corpus. The whole corpus contains 256 (2^8) chapters. The chapters have names which are exactly the same as the names ascribed to the pattern printed on the

---

[1] Wande Abimbola, *Sixteen Great Poems of Ifa*. (New York: UNESCO, 1975): 3.
[2] ibid.
[3] Wande Abimbola, *Ifa Divination Poetry*. (Lagos: NOK Publisher, 1977), pp. 4 - 9.

powder of divination when the sixteen sacred palm-nuts are used for divination. For example, when all eight nuts present their inside surface upward, that pattern is known as *Eji ogbe* and when they present their outside surface, the signature is that of *oyeku Meji*.[4]

The Ifa priest keeps track of divination by making marks on the divination powder contained in the divining tray. The tray itself bears carved images of animals typical of the fauna of the Yoruba world. The most important carved object on the tray is the image of Esu, the Yoruba trickster god. Abimbola describes the divining tray graphically:

> The divining tray is carved into different shapes and sizes. The edges of each tray are dominated by intricate patterns of different objects such as birds, reptiles, tortoises, and wild animals. The middle of the top section is usually reserved for the image of *Èsù* (the trickster divinity who keeps the *àse*). From this position, the image of *Èsù* faces the Ifa priest as if he is directing or watching the divination exercise.[5]

Ifa divination is marked by a series of chants from specific chapters of Ifa poetry. The corpus is multi-generic, showing a wide variety of forms like anecdotes, wits, dilemma poems and tales told in poetry. These genres are connected in their reflection of patterns of conflicts and resolution through sacrifices. In actual divination, the Ifa priest continues his chant till the client tells him he has found the verse, which bears the story that relates to his own problem. The priest then prescribes the same sacrifices contained in the verse that the client has identified.

Certain significant aesthetic *phenomena* emerge from the Ifa complex. One finds that the basic function of poetry within this oral mode of production is to resolve everyday human problems. Aesthetic currents still play out even in the context of the sacred ritualism of divination as priest and client relate in drawing meanings from the stock of Ifa poetry. This admixture of the ritualistic and the aesthetic is noted by Soyinka in his description of Ifa as a cycle of Masonic poetry which is prognostic, aesthetic and omniscient expressing a profound philosophy of optimism in its oracular adaptiveness and unassailable resolution of all *phenomena*.[6] The Ifa corpus embraces certain internal symbolic essences, which are useful to a writer seeking materials to construct a model social vision. As argued earlier, Ifa is a complex of plural aesthetic and ideational forces containing poetry of all kinds and tales rendered in dramatic

---

[4] Wande Abimbola, *Ifa Divination Poetry*: 6.
[5] ibid: 9.
[6] Wole Soyinka, *Myth Literature and the African World*. (London: Cambridge University Press, 1978): 155.

form. The corpus also embodies the cultural values and vision of a people and places itself as the most enduring intellectual and philosophical symbol of the Yoruba world-view. The aesthetic and cultural pluralism noticed in Ifa point to the dynamism of the corpus. As Olu Obafemi puts it, this dynamism

> comes out in its being at the root of other forms of Yoruba oral literature including *iwi* (poetry of *Egungun*), *oriki* (praise poetry connected with lineages and origins), *Ijala* (poetry used for professional rituals and ceremonies of hunters, farmers and blacksmiths- all devotees of Ogun), all of which form a wide range of knowledge that emerges from non-literate society. This knowledge stored in Ifa literature exists in contemporary Nigerian society.[7]

Images and icons within the Ifa corpus show the dialectical interrelation of forces. Ifa's association with Esu, the trickster god portrays this dialectical struggle of opposites. We have already noted that Esu, who dispenses chaos occupies the centre of the Ifa divination tray. Of course, this means that knowledge requires constant disruption and rupture to create new forms of consciousness and vision.

Launko's transfer of materials from the Ifa corpus occurs in two ways. First, *Dream-Seeker on Divining Chain* contains ritual refrains signalized in songs, chants, icons and other referents associated with Ifa corpus. Connected with these forms are the tales which occur as allegories and therefore serve to communicate the essential principles which the artist borrows for the purpose interpreting and humanizing his environment. Second, the poet connects black activists, singers and indeed, all politically active art-producers with the Ifa principle of mediation and reconstruction. These figures are cast in the text as seekers of knowledge; the Ifa incarnates those who recommend selfless service and sacrifice as the means to make society grow. This symbolic connection of contemporary mediators with the deity of knowledge underlines the nature of the social concern in Launko's *Dream-Seeker on Divining Chain*.

Myth and Inferences

In the dramatic opening lines of *Dream-Seeker on Divining Chain*, the poet enacts a spectacle in which the ritual icons of Ifa divination convey a quest that is both spiritual and aesthetic. The quest manifests in the symbols of the divination tray, "the yellow sands", "the chain of sacred nuts", "the carved ivory

---

[7] Olu Obafemi, *Contemporary Nigerian Theatre: Cultural Heritage and Social Vision*. (Bayreuth African Studies, Vol. 40, Bayreuth 1996): 243.

rattle" and "the stone." These objects relate to set the beginning of a quest, a dream or a journey into the terrains of social and aesthetic intervention:

> Set the tray down:
>
> Across her face, spread the yellow sands
> like a woman's, polished for a tryst ...
>
> (& this dream will be starting...)
>
> Now, with deft hand,
> throw the chain of sacred nuts:
>
> The poet is ready:
> in his hand, the carved ivory rattle, the stone...[8]

From this invocative beginning, one draws the inference that knowledge is the reward of a search but this also entails sacrifice. Hence, the poet chants:

> Riru ebo nii gbeni
> Airu ebo kii gbeniyan...
>
> Iwaju, iwaju
> lopa ebiti resi
> iwaju iwaju...
>
> (It is sacrifice that attracts benefits
> And the lack of it impedes blessings...
>
> Forward, ever forward
> trips the lever of the rabbit-trap
> forward, ever forward.)[9]

The poet takes the role of the diviner in a voyage into discovery. Of course, this role calls for the appropriation of the most sacred ritual elements: the Ifa tray in which the divination powder is spread, the sacred nuts used only for highly ritualistic purposes and other instruments which attend the spiritual and aesthetic quest. The search requires invocation and sacrificial offers. The poet's journey is for peace and love, and so he invokes Yoruba pantheon figures connected with love and healing:

> O Oya, we invoke you!
> Yeye Osun, watermelon of fecund seeds!

---

[8] Okinba Launko, *Dream-Seeker on Divining Chain*. (Ibadan: Kraft Books Ltd., 1993): 14. All subsequent page references are made to this edition.

[9] This is the poet's own translation: 14.

> and Iwapele, wife of my father,
> favourite of the Father of secrets!
>
> We have come neither for stillness
> nor the flash of the axe- *Sango Olukoso o*!
>
> but only for love and for healing (p. 15)

Sacrifice is vital to Ifa divination and conflict resolution rests on attracting the divinities and the ancestors with offerings specified by the priest. In *Dream-Seeker on Divining Chain*, the poet's many-sided journey requires sacrificial offers to illuminate his passage and to integrate him with the spiritual and artistic sources, which inspire his creativity. His sacrificial items symbolize peace, life and creativity and the purpose is to cleanse his passage:

> Here, clear water.
> Here, kola nuts. A basketful of sand.
> Blood of a snail.
> The head of a tortoise:
> I add my guitar, my xylophone: (p. 15)

The poet creates the scene of pantheon invocation and the images of weaverbirds and bees reveal the poet-protagonist pleading for a creative voice, "words [that] shall not stumble." (p. 15)

In at least two poems, Launko demonstrates the values, which inhere in the myth of Ifa by a creative transposition of certain texts in the corpus. The first few line in "Orunmila's treasure" are written in the fast swinging mode of Ifa chant:

> It was If-Advance-Is-Impossible,
> The-Back-Is-There-For-Retreat, blood brother of
> The-Homestead-Is-Always-Ready-To-
> Welcome-Back-The-Trueborn-If-He-Has-to-Flee,
> Or-If-He-Wearies-Of-Wandering,
> Who threw the chain of nuts for Agbonniregun,
> Leader of cults, on the day he sat downcast
> Somewhere in the corner of one European autumn
> His mind drifting with the dead leaves adrift around him,
> Dying with the death dancing everywhere like a chameleon
> in confusing sounds and colorful disguises. (p. 84)

The poet examines the exile phenomenon, which ensnares many African intellectuals. The lines are reconstructed wits from the Ifa corpus. These wits are used to support the theme of voyage and the wisdom is that when a journey reaches a dead-end, it is time for homecoming. Often, this return turns into hidden gifts, the "Orunmila treasure" which modernity suppresses. In the poem,

31

three objects are presented as symbolic gifts; treasures, which are neglected yet they play crucial role in building society:

>The *ado*, replied Orunmila, is a calabash of herbs:
>They say it carries the powders which turn words into
>prayer, and bring healing to all woes and wounds-

>The *àse* is this ivory carving in my hand
>A touch of it on the tongue, they say, and words acquire
>The aura of magic, and do exactly as they are told-

>And the *eso* is what they say you slide under the tongue
>To sweeten thoughts into melodies, and win by song
>And suasion even the hardiest antagonists! (p. 85)

A similar pattern of symbols also occurs in "Ifa and the Hunter". Here, again, the hunter's quest attended with dogs, guns and cutlass provokes death and destruction. The Ifa essence of harmony and love, symbolized in the poem by a flute and a beautiful woman are won by shedding the paraphernalia of war and violence. The poet recommends the Ifa virtues of creativity and service as the redeeming agents of social transformation. The poem is significant for emphasizing in symbols the humanizing power of the creative-intellectual personality as opposed to the killing mentality of the man of the gun. The poet asks rhetorically:

>Of what use is a gun
>Besides the eloquent power of a flute
>Or the euphonious fountain of a pen? (p. 100)

Contemporary Mediators

Launko's book presents poetic figures and experiences that are shaped by the creative-intellectual essences of the Ifa complex. In tradition, Ifa is regarded as a molder, one who tends the world with his great knowledge. This role is canonized in Ifa verses as the following divination poem indicates:

>Pa, bi osan ja
>Osan ja,
>Awo won lode Itori;
>Akatanpo jakun,
>O dobiiri kale,
>A dia fun Orunmila
>Ifa nlo taye Oluufe, oro, so
>Bi eni ti nsobga
>Ta ni o waa ba ni

> Tayee wa wonyi so?
> Ewe opepe tile so.
> Orunmila ni oowaa ba ni
> Tayee wa wonyi so,
> Ewe opepe tile so.
>
> (Sudden as the snap of leader string,
> Leather-string-snaps,
> Their Ifa priest in the of Itori.
> When akatanpo loses its ground.
> Ifa divination was performed for Orunmila
> When he was going to mend the life of the king of Ife
> As one mends broken calabash.
> Who then will help us
> Mend our lives?
> It is Orunmila who will help us
> Mend our lives.
> The palm-tree grows leaves from its tender age.[10]

The committed artists, the singer, the political activists whose experiences we follow in *Dream-Seeker on Divining Chain* are involved in mending society, like Ifa, whose sacred duty is to mediate in conflicts. Ngugi Wa Thiong'o, Okot p'Bitek, Wole Soyinka and Don Mattera are some of the names celebrated in Launko's poetry. Like Ifa, these people are seekers of knowledge. They are intellectuals who are active and interested in social organization and political reconstruction.

In "Find Iwapele", Launko emphasizes the notion that a commitment to the task of creativity is the enduring alternative to "the corrupting touch of the money baron" (p. 128). Iwapele, the exemplar of patience and vision becomes the poet's creative Muse.[11] The poet's association with Iwa (Ifa's wife) is a symbol of the search for the most desirable unity with the source of creativity and grace. As noted earlier, the Ifa complex presents an example of a dialectical interplay of forces. Soyinka for instance points out that this dialectical relation, particularly the balance of opposing forces, is the core of Ifa oracular wisdom.[12]

---

[10] Wande Abimbola, *Ifa Divination Poetry*: 56-57.

[11] See Rowland Abiodun, "The Future of African Art Studies: An African Perspective". Paper presented at a Symposium organized by the National Museum of African Art, Smithsonian Institution (Washington DC: National Museum of African Art, 1990): 63-89. Abiodun's discussion locates the virtues of Iwapele within the Yoruba world view and there is the argument that the artist needs Iwapele's grace, insight and composed gait in advocating for desirable social form.

[12] Wole Soyinka, *Myth Literature and the African World*. (London: Cambridge University Press, 1978): 156.

In the poem, "Parting", Launko demonstrates that nature's values exist in dialectical opposition. The intellectuals, with their gift of knowledge must exploit these contradictions in nature to humanize their environment: "Ours to discover them:/ours also to multiply them" (p. 25). The poet lends us the insight that society derives its stability from the discovery of the "antidote" and the "plenitude" for social construction.

In the poem titled "Tomorrow", the poet expresses the social function of the creative intellectual. Two contrasting classes are set in combat here. The creative man confronts the army general with his own weapon, the poem. The poet takes the reader through the network of state apparatuses of power and coercion. We hear of the exclusive password into the power domain and the propaganda machinery of repression. The poet sets the difference between the soldier and the poet. The army General destroys with the gun but the artist, like Ifa, uses his text (the poem) to humanize:

> I shall pass by the beggar and
> the go-slows
> blowing the only siren I have: my poem...
> I warn, floating without paddles
> in the season's flood of decrees, of songs
> Which are green but hiss like snakes.
> I say that the moment has come to
> dig our roots far
> from forest fire, from the acid
> of wayward tongues. (p. 57)

Launko celebrates the resilience of the intellectual and creative genius in performing the task of social construction. In "Gani's Daughter", the poet uses the symbols of placards and bullets to make a distinction between the warrior personality and the political activist. The poet proposes the principles of research and creativity as valid means of building a society and recommends sustained critical voices against "the stubborn ears of corrupt power" (p. 106).

The correlation between the contemporary mediators and Ifa, molder of the earth, may be viewed more closely by considering the problems which may arise as a result of their physical disengagement from the premise of mediation. Their disengagement as a result of incarceration or exile creates a void in normal social functioning. Of course, this has a parallel in the Ifa myth on organic decay, social chaos and the plague of sterility following Ifa's exile from earth:

> Aboyun o bi mo
> Agan o towo bosun.
> Okunrin o dide.
> Akeremodo o wewu irawe.

Ato gbe mo omokunrin ni idi;
Obinrin o ri asee re mo.
Isu peyin o ta;
Agbado tape o gbo;
Eree yoju opolo.
Ojo paapaapaa kan sile,
Ewure mu un je.

(Pregnant women could not deliver their babies;
Barren women remained barren.
Small river were covered up with fallen leaves.
Semen dried in men's testicles
Women no longer saw their menstruation.
Yam formed small but undeveloped tubers;
Corn grew small but unripened ears.
Scattered drops of rain fell down,
Chicken attempted to eat them up:
Well-sharpened razor were placed on the floor,
And goats attempted to devour them.)[13]

    Totalitarianism is a real challenge to the creative mind and the activist-intellectual. This manifests in the despot's creation of conditions of alienation and exile. Launko treats this problem in "Exile Song." Here, the exile of contemporary mediators from the poet's society holds social life into a stand-still. These conditions, especially the deliberate alienation of the true intellectuals from the state define the essence of Launko's intervention through a poetic kind that seeks vision from Ifa pool of creativity and knowledge.

---

[13] Wande Abimbola, *Ifa Divination Poetry*: 3.

IV. ORAL ART FORMS AND SOCIAL VISION IN THE POETRY OF NIYI OSUNDARE AND JACK MAPANJE

With Osundare and Mapanje, the relation with orature is informed by the more demanding purpose of constructing coherent modes to articulate their vision. In their individual works, both poets express their aversion to the pervasive atmosphere of state terror and repression around them. Osundare raises alarm against what he describes as the "overwhelming physicality of [the tyrant's] weapon and strategies of violence"[1] and restates the role of literature in this circumstance:

> And how can literature help to conquer that fear, rupture that silence, and neutralize that violence? By constantly, intelligently exposing the lies at the root of every violence; the lies which feeds and strengthens it.[2]

The oral art has a role in this engagement and the purpose in this section of the study is to examine Osundare's *Village Voices* and Jack Mapanje's *Of Chameleons and the Gods* in order to find out the ways in which major oral forms like songs, icons, dirges and myths are employed to construct their vision.

Fables, Wits and Poetic Mediation

Needless to say, oral forms have their own existence and functions within the culture. They are often used in written literature to perform similar functions. The act of correlating the artistic and social functions of existing oral genres with creative possibilities in written poetry for instance, makes sense because these forms have succeeded through the ages in conditioning certain valuable means of cognizing and humanizing the society. Daniel P. Kunene expresses related views in his argument that allegory, parables and other genres

> ... can be seen as a continuation of the tradition of oral narrative, particularly of the use of the fable as a commentary on human affairs. Allegory owes its effectiveness perhaps largely to the fact that some commonly accepted experiences of life, with their related consequences or associations, are used as a

---

[1] Niyi Osundare, "Freedom and the Creative Space". *ALA Bulletin: A Publication of the African Literature Association* 24, 2 (Spring 1998): 54.
[2] ibid.

surface argument for closely parallel situation which would seem to be incontrovertible once the surface or illustrating argument is accepted.[3]

It is fascinating to trace the ways in which African poets across different regions seize on their oral sources to reflect similar social themes. For instance, Osundare uses the fable on chicken to raise questions on the compensatory order of nature:

> Who does the chicken think
> it is deceiving?
> It eats pebbles
> and swallows sands
> yet complains of toothlessness
> the goat which has teeth
> the dog which fortifies its mouth
> with the strongest of ivory
> dare they eat pebbles in the morning
> and still walk about at noon?[4]

In Mapanje's poetry, folkloric elements like fable and wits are used to express experiences and to extend meanings. In "Song of the Chickens" for instance, fable and wit are employed to expose the ambiguity in human actions. As a fable, the poem relies on the critical voice of the animal figure to create effect:

> Master, you talked with bows,
> Arrows and catapults once
> Your hands steaming with hawk blood
> To protect your chicken.
>
> Why do you talk with knives now,
> Your hands teaming with eggshells
> And hot blood from your own chicken?
> Is it to impress your visitors?[5]

This fable form accommodates metaphors and wits, which allow for a wide range of interpretations. One of such is the ambivalent position of certain political figures in dealing with the crucial question of leadership in Africa. Mapanje alludes to the tragic irony in which the freedom fighters of yesteryears,

---

[3] Daniel P. Kunene, "The Crusading Writer, his Modes, Themes and Styles" in Mineke Schipper-de Leeuw (ed.), *Text and Context: Methodological Exploration in the Field of African Literature*. (Leiden: African Studies Centrum, 1976): 107.

[4] Niyi Osundare, *Village Voices*. (Ibadan: Evans Brothers Ltd., 1984): 14. Subsequent page references are made to this edition and occur in the text.

[5] Jack Mapanje, *Of Chameleons and the Gods*. (London: Heinemann, 1981): 4. All subsequent page references are made to this edition and appear in the text.

who "talked with bows and catapults" (p. 4) to liberate the land from colonial hold, now "talk with knives" of plunder against the same land.

Icons, Images and Meaning-making

Osundare and Mapanje show their concern for the contradictions that exist between city life and the rural, bucolic tradition. The dichotomy is often used as a metaphor for the decadence and affluence of the ruling elite as against the communal but impoverished agrarian people.

Although we find in *Village Voices* (especially in "Akintunde Come Home") the romanticist metaphor of the city as a destroyer, Osundare's picture of village life is not in any way idealized, if for example, we define the term in the sense and spirit of the Wordsworthian romanticism in a poem like "Michael". Images in "Akintunde Come Home" show a village of natural disaster inhabited by the exploited poor:

>   Come back here
>   where the walls are mud
>   and meatless meals quiet
>   the howling stomach
>   come back here
>   where dreams spun on campaign promises
>   snap in the noisy bellies
>   of belching parliaments
>
>   come home son,
>   through our thatched roofs
>   we can see the devouring deluge
>   of looming clouds. (pp. 22-23)

Osundare engages the metaphor of racing and the symbol of a monster city to express the devouring savage culture of modern life:

>   Akintunde, I have told you to come,
>   come home from the land
>   where life is a race in which
>   the strong trample the weak, dashing
>   for the fluttering fragments
>   of stolen trophies
>   come away from bubbles
>   which melt like wax
>   before a raging blaze. (p. 22)

In this poem, meaning-making depends strongly on creative deployment of images and icons borrowed from the oral art. The *Iroko* tree, which is an icon in many Yoruba rituals and poetry is employed here to portray a power rage in which the weak becomes the sacrificial object:

> Come home, son,
> for we cannot be all iroko
> slapping the sky's face
> with imperious boughs
> while the lower forest
> dies a sunless death
> at our unfeeling feet
> come away from the fold
> of sun stealers. (p. 22)

The *Iroko* icon, within the context of the *Ifa* poetic corpus, reveals the allegory of serious life struggle involving sacrifices and conquests. Osundare's imaginative transfer connects this oral art in form and content as the following example collected by Wande Abimbola indicates:

> Awon ota ni nda Iroko laamu ...
> Won ni ebo ni ki o waa ru
> Igba ti o rubo tan
> Ni esu ba loo pe awon agbe wa
> Pe ki won o maa san igbo
> Ti Iroko mbe ninuu re
> Gbogbo awon igi ti mba Iroko sota
> Ni awon agbe be lule.
> Igba ti won de idi Iroko,
> Esu niwon ko gbodo ge e
> Nitori pe igi abami ni.
> (Enemies were worrying the Iroko tree of the city of Igbo...
> He was told to perform sacrifices,...
> After he had performed sacrifices,
> Esu went and called farmers,
> And ordered them to start clearing the forest
> Inside which the Iroko tree was.
> All the trees which were the enemies of Iroko
> Were cut down by the farmers.
> But when they got to the foot of the Iroko tree,
> Esu commanded that they must not cut him
> Because he was not an ordinary tree.)[6]

---

[6] Wande Abimbola, *Ifa Divination Poetry*. (New York: NOK Publishers Ltd., 1977): 76-77.

Of course, Osundare's picture of contemporary life in the African context comes out more graphically in the framework of borrowed oral forms. These materials transfer the qualities of their own imagery to influence meanings in the poems they inhabit.

One finds in Mapanje's poetry a similar reflection. The poem, "Messages" (in *Of Chameleons and the Gods*) expresses the problem of the decay of city life and its consuming effect on the village youth. Both Osundare and Mapanje employ the technique of the collective voice indicating the communal vision typical of traditional social and aesthetic practices. In Mapanje's "Messages" for instance, a mother speaks in riddles and in a collective voice to condemn her daughter's adoption of city life:

> Tell
> Her besides, a cat sees best at night
> Not much at noon and so when time
> Comes, while she eats and drinks
> While she twists and shouts, rides
> And travels, we shall refuse
> To reach her our stuff of fortune
> Even if she called us witches!
> We swear by our fathers dead! (p. 14)

Here, the "stuff of fortune" is a mother's traditional gift to a daughter symbolizing and acknowledging filial piety. Mapanje weaves this icon into poetry to express two levels of disconnection: the girl's disconnection with her traditional origin and then, in a more specific sense, the severance of the tie with her life source, in this case, her mother. The poet's description reflects the typical image of the archetypal ruined maid:

> Her back swirls off me
> Gassed by reeking perfumes, sitting:
> Tattering curtains, doors to bathrooms
> Couples in corners unabashed
>
> She comes back thick-lip-cigaretted
> The chest jutting into the world generously
> The lashes greased bluer. (p. 14)

She looses the opportunity of a link (through the speaker) and darts off "floating to the next customer" (p. 15) unable to respond to 'her navel' name, Asawilunda. This action, rendered in the technique of drama-in-poetry, expresses the girl's decadent and fragmented self.

Except in their choice of oral forms which are specific and uniquely tied up to their individual region, there is no major difference between Osundare and

Mapanje in their use of the oral art to express the phenomenon of urban decay. In "Messages", Mapanje contrasts the city and the village using the images of hunting and war. Images reveal the survival of the communal values of the traditional set up even within the most competitive context:

> Did you think it was a hunting party
> Where after a fall from chasing a hare
> You laughed together an enemy shaking
> Dust off your bottom, a friend reaching
> You your bow and arrow? (p. 15)

The city is pictured as an arena of battle where everyone wages "a lonely war" (p. 15) to "hack [his] own way single-handed/To make anything up to the Shaka of/The tribe!" (p. 15). Like the *Iroko* icon in Osundare's "Akintunde Come Home", the Shaka symbol in Mapanje's "Messages" works intertextually, connecting the Zulu epic on Shaka to amplify meanings. In other words, the referent, Shaka, evokes an existing oral poetic form (an epic), part of which Mapanje and Landeg White include in their book of oral poetry:

> Ferocious one of the Mbelebe brigade,
> Who raged among the large kraals,
> So that until dawn the huts were being turned upside down...
> He who beats but is not beaten, unlike water,
> Axe that surpasses other axes in sharpness;
> Shaka, I fear to say he is Shaka,
> Shaka, he is the chief of the Mashobas.
> He who armed in the forest, who is like a madman,...
> He who while devouring some devoured others
> And as he devoured others he devoured some more.[7]

This epic symbol (as used in "Messages") affects the poem with the meanings it bears in the original epic, part of which is the struggle for domination in the world of warlords. In a more political sense, this may just be Mapanje's cryptic response to the devouring politics of the Banda era.

Songs, Dirges, Myths and Aesthetic Mediation

Songs, dirges and myths occur in Niyi Osundare's poetry as transferred items used creatively to comment on contemporary social situations. As argued earlier, the functions that these genres perform in oral culture are sustained in the written texts into which they are transferred. Speaking about the value of the

---

[7] Jack Mapanje and Landeg White, *Oral Poetry from Africa*. (New York: Longman, 1983): 25-26.

song, Osundare casts the broad perspective in which the song manifests itself in the oral context:

> Traditional, oral Africa thrives on the song; every occasion has its lyrics, even trivial incidents provoke a ballad. There are songs which mark the inexorable cycle of human existence - birth, puberty, marriage age, and death. There are songs for praising, songs for cursing, songs of abuse; songs which wax purple in the king's palace, ... The town crier talks in song, ... I have seen old people weep in poetry ...[8]

In Osundare's *Village Voices*, song is employed as a medium for biting satirical lashes against the corrupt ("Not in my Season of Song") and for raising social consciousness ("The Prisoner's Song"). There are at least two levels of creative transfer of songs. There is a physical transfer, which involves the use of songs in their original indigenous forms. This mode of transfer is often accompanied with what Osundare himself calls 'mediated translation'. This song type provides rhythm and added meanings especially when the poem is rendered as a performance. The following song, taken from Osundare's *Waiting Laughters* (1990) illustrates this kind of transfer:

> Omi i lo o, iyanrin lookun rode
> Omi i lo o, Iyanrin lookun rode
> Aye mo re de, e emee jemi lo loona o o o
>
> (The water is going
> Going going going
> The water is going)[9]

The song expands the themes of the dialectics of motion and stillness; the passage of time, history and the perseverance of those who convert these agencies into new forms of social commitment. In the main poem, images are structured to convey the opposing classes of visionary creators who, like rare flowers, "cling, still,/To the beard of the valley/... dancing in the whistling wind" (p. 67) and visionless men who "sharpen dark knives/For our fledgling voice" (p. 67). The poet constructs moral justice in the model of a life taker becoming "drowned in the deluge of the echoes" of "A village of rolling hills" (p. 67). The song brings out the deeper meanings of the poem for its images and sense are analogous with the intended message of the poem. So, what the song does is to illuminate by replication.

---

[8] Niyi Osundare, "Bard of the Tabloid Platform: A Personal Experience of Newspaper Poetry in Nigeria". Canadian Association of African Studies Conference, Edmonton, Alberta, Canada (1987): 11.

[9] Niyi Osundare, *Waiting Laughters*. (Lagos: Malthouse Press Ltd., 1990): 67. Subsequent page references are made to this edition and occur in the text.

The other level of transfer of songs works through the technique of close translation, a mode that Aderemi Bamikunle finds to be basic to the composition of "The Prisoner's Song" (in *Village Voices*).[10] Osundare uses this technique in "The Bridal Song". The poem is a direct rendering of the traditional bridal song, which normally incorporates oral genres like praise poetry and the lament to present the theme of departure. In mood and imagery, Osundare's English rendering is close to the original:

> Baba, thank you today
> For the kindness of many years
> Going am I now to my husband
> The son of Efurudowo whose yams
> Wrestle heaps to the ground
> Owner of the powerful machete
> Whose maize drills the molars
> Like seasoned warriors
> My calabash tray will give way
> Coming back from his farm. (p. 42)

The choice of this genre makes sense against the background of the decaying of values signified in Osundare's "Akintunde, Come Home" and Mapanje's "Messages". The poetic figure in "The Bridal Song" symbolizes moral virtues and therefore functions as an alternative to the lost child archetype in both "Akintunde, Come Home" and "Messages".

There is a slightly different mode of transfer in Osundare's "A Dialogue of the Drum". Here, Osundare creates a performance atmosphere with voices of poet-singers, audience and the sound of the drums. The poet defines his origin in terms of songs and drums:

> I hail from a line of drummers ...
> I was born with a song in my throat
> And my hands on the face of the drum...
> Whatever song you raise
> Is what the world sings after you. (p. 6)

Osundare exploits the traditional performance atmosphere of poetic exchanges between two poets to define the nature of his art. He distances himself from the palace singer whose drum is "dumb in the marketplace" and whose royal song "extol those whose words/Behead the world" (p. 7). The song and the drum, for the poet, become meaningful only when they are employed to tell the truth, "the fangs of facts" (p. 7) even as state violence is visited on the

---

[10] See Aderemi Bamikunle, "Niyi Osundare's Poetry and the Yoruba Oral Artistic Tradition". *African Literature Today* 18 (1992): 56.

artist to silence him. Osundare insists that the great task of the artist is in sustaining "the audacity to keep telling the emperor: "Your majesty, thou, indeed, art naked" even as tyrannical rulers "send dissident writers to the gallows with ... medieval equanimity".[11]

In "A Dialogue of the Drums", Osundare recreates the confrontational atmosphere typical of the traditional song-of-abuse to cast a diatribe against the artist who jettisons critical intervention to take up the role of a palace artist:

> Where were you when adan filled the night
> With the shame of Apeloko
> Who proved too sharp with the neighbour's yams?
> I know where you were ...
> You were in the palace, running endless errands
> Your eunuch drum a dumb stool
> For harem buttocks (p. 7)

The poet's vision is tied up with the plight of the ordinary people. He sees in them a more consistent value and inspiration which "always outlast the palace" (p. 8) and to be on their side is to unite with the most stable arena of creativity.

The dirge form appears in *Village Voices* and the best example is "The Star Sob". This poem is a close translation of the Yoruba dirge:

> You who kill kings
> as if they had no crowns
> you who snatch the rich
> like beggars hauled from
> a heap of backstreet garbage
> you who kill a physician
> as if his art were a moonlight trick (p. 35)

As the following example shows, traditional dirge emphasizes the sense of loss by locating parallel images of death in nature:

> Ko seni ti o ni dale bora ninuu wa
> B'eruun ba yan,
> Gbogbo kooko a keru, a re 'wale aja.
> (Without exception, everyone shall make a wrapper of
>   ground.
> When dry season is severe,
> All grasses shall pack up and die.)[12]

---

[11] Niyi Osundare, "Freedom and the Creative Space": 53.
[12] Bade Ajuwon, *Funeral Dirges of Yoruba Hunters*. (Lagos: NOK Publishers International, 1982): 59.

Osundare translates this relation of art and ecology into a creative force and this reflects in "The Star Sob":

> you who go up a tree
> coming down with the juiciest fruit
> Ah! the stars are sobbing
>
> Forests drop their tuft of green
> vegetables go pale
> on the market stall (p. 36.)

In "An Elegy for Mangochi Fishermen", Mapanje employs the dirge form to express collective loss. He uses the symbol of a capsized canoe to mediate on and lament the death of a tradition:

> The virgin canoe we once boasted about
> Holding the head or pushing the rear
> Pulling the lips or rolling on poles,
> The canoe has capsized, the carvers drowned. (p. 69)

Mapanje physicalizes death by constructing images of motion, which decay progressively. We hear of "the muscles/Twitching with power" (p. 69) and "the husky voices chanting" (p. 69) but then, come the images of darkness and death in the lines: "the vigil wax has melted away" (p. 69), "the light is out"(p. 69) and "in our cryptic recesses/We must all lie in pitch dark stakes" (p. 69). Of course, there is a serious political statement in the dirge for the dying situation of things points to a national tragedy.

Quite often, Osundare uses Yoruba myths to build up ideas. In *Waiting Laughters* for instance, he imagines a revolutionary situation in which the people, fed up with the "garnished sand from the kitchen/of heartless season" (p. 22) take the "screaming stone" (p. 22) and "the humble axe" (p. 22) to terminate the reign of a tyrant. There is a vision of revolt in Osundare's allusion to *Orogodo*, an *Ikere* (Yoruba) myth, which he describes as "a remote place of banishment for dishonorable rulers" (p. 22):

> Behold the wonder,
> the crown is only a cap!
>
> Orogododo Orogodo...
> Oba ba ti beyi
> O'mo d'Orogododo o o o o
>
> The king's brave legs are bone and flesh ...
> The castle is a house of mortar and stone (p. 22)

The lines unravel the powerlessness of the king or ruler once he loses the people's support. Furthermore, the myth is used to indicate a new possibility, which is the capacity of the ordinary people to recover their inherent collective force, a phenomenon, which is stronger than the power of a ruler. Osundare sustains this pattern of demystification in his poetry, borne here by the metaphor of discovery, which reflects in the line, "the crown is only a cap!" This kind of pattern bears the imprint of the radical vision in Osundare's poetry.

As Mapanje declares, *Of Chameleon and Gods* emerges from the ambience of a political set up in which "personal voices are too easily muffled".[13] The use of the cryptic mode, indeed the adoption of the chameleon camouflage is understandable. One expects to find in Mapanje's poetry a subtle approach to myth in reflecting the chaos of the Malawian society under Banda. His much read "Glory Be to Chingwe's Hole" bears such reflection. In this poem, two separate but related myths are employed to capture the theme of repression. Chingwe's Hole refers to the hole on the Zomba plateau in Malawi. It has acquired the property of a myth.[14] As a stone dungeon, it connects archetypes like the Sophoclean life burial in stone and the death-cells of contemporary prisons in countries under the siege of despots. Chingwe Hole is a symbol of horror. It devours victims "bundled up in sacks/Alive "(p. 44). This myth connects the Chewa myth which tells the story of a king who abducts the wife of a carver.[15] Beauty, as the myth goes, is the wife of Frog, the carver whose art led to the creation of Beauty. The myth, as used by Mapanje, unravels the telling irony of the despot-beast who finds it desirable to acquire beauty, the product of the artist he seeks to destroy.

It is important to mention that the proverb is a vital sub-genre to meaning-making in Osundare's poetry. Osundare uses this oral form to achieve a more coherent articulation of vision. There is an interesting relation of the form to the setting in "A Villager's Protest", where a villager speaks in proverbs, the form he is most acquainted with to express his anger against corrupt politicians:

>Esuru grows swollen-headed
>and outgrows the prestigious belly
>of the mortar
>the wasp power-stung
>enters a race of waists

---

[13] see, Jack Mapanje, (Introduction) *Of Chameleons and Gods*: xi.
[14] ibid: 77.
[15] ibid: 77-78.

> Men of deep unwisdom
> knowing not that
> power is the bird of the forest
> which nests on one tree today
> and tomorrow pitches its tent
> on another. (p. 48)

As creative products, oral art forms have their own re-creative force and the kind of adaptability that will always make them, to use Osundare's words "persist without greying"[16] It appears the difference between Osundare and Mapanje lies in the extent to which ideology impacts on the aesthetic. Osundare's poetry is informed by a discernable revolutionary vision what Biodun Jeyifo describes as "poetry of revolution and a revolution in poetry".[17] This is of course evident in Osundare's appropriation of oral aesthetics to mediate in politics. With Mapanje, it is not the voice of the ideologue-poet that we hear but a subtle voice, camouflaged in images drawn from oral sources but one that still tugs at the very heart of despots.

---

[16] Niyi Osundare, "Bard of the Tabloid Platform: A Personal Experience of Newspaper Poetry in Nigeria": 3.

[17] Biodun Jeyifo, Introduction to Niyi Osundare, *Songs of the Marketplace*. (Ibadan: New Horn Press, 1987):xi.

V. ORAL AESTHETIC AND THE AFRICAN EXPERIENCE: THE POETRY OF OKELLO OCULI

Okello Oculi's poetry is inspired by the oral tradition of his Northern Ugandan grassland background as well as an aesthetic tradition which invests written poetry with oral voice and other techniques. In the particular case of literary influence, it is appropriate to relate Oculi's poetry to the p'Bitekian type[24], which, as the discussion on p'Bitek shows reflect the techniques of oral poetry.

Speaking of East African poetry, Oculi offers that p'Bitek's art and vision set the pace especially in incorporating the performance forms of "singing and dancing by the rural artist."[25] He describes p'Bitek's *Song of Lawino* as "an instant success throughout East Africa" and emphasizes, "if there was any sense of bubbling creativity in East Africa, Okot p'Bitek was really the main spring board... The success of *Song of Lawino* was so much that it was able to carry the burden of so many other books."[26] Of course, what Oculi also alludes to here is that the text continues to inspire other texts and one of such texts is *Orphan*, where Oculi experiments with the oral narrative voice and other techniques derived from oral traditions. These other techniques are songs, dance and the drama-in-poetry mode that generates interplay of actions and relations between the orphan (the major poetic figure) and the various people who attempt to mediate upon him.

The Dramatic and the Oral Narrative Forms

Evidence of the dramatic form within the poetic mode reflects in the prologue mode, which Oculi introduces to set the performance base of the poetry:

> You are going to watch a village opera performed. You will see
> each character walking along a path. All paths crisscross at a junction.
> An orphan boy is seated cross-legged at the junction, writing pictures

---

[24] see D. I. Nwoga, "Modern African Poetry: The Domestication of a Tradition". *African Literature Today* 10, (1979): 47. Here, Nwoga makes a brief comment on the poetry of Oculi and relates his art with that of p'Bitek.

[25] Charles Bodunde, "Interview with Okello Oculi". *Tape Recording* 13th March 1999 Fez, Morocco.

[26] ibid.

>of animals in the sand. He is pensive. Today the people who
>talk in these pages all pass through this junction. Each of them notices
>the orphan boy. In the village the problem of unnoticing is still minimal.
>Each person performs a drama for the orphan boy, and all of them with
>the orphan boy perform for you and me.[27]

Given the fixed nature of aesthetic modes, one may consider this prologue format as inappropriate as a prelude to poetry. However, what Oculi does with this technique is to demonstrate that the African aesthetic is rather more elastic in terms of aesthetic modes and genres. In other words, Oculi uses the slim prologue to display the range of possibilities, which inhere in the total art (multi-genre) tradition of the African aesthetic. As Oculi explains in the text, this kind of synthesis reflects the nature of oral aesthetic production:

> To those that feel that the decorum of poetry has been infringed in parts of this poem, I can only say I would feel guilty if I backed away from a natural force that is part of the essence of the outpouring of the African mind.(p. 9)

The dialogic mode reflects in a number of the poems in *Orphan*. The various sections of the book constitute a whole entity representing a drama of the experience of the orphan character. As the poet indicates, in the prologue, these sections present characters whose (dramatic) actions impinge on the orphan and the reader or audience. Each section contains dialogic indexes, which establish relations between the orphan and these other mediating characters. For instance in the section titled "grandmother of Okello's father's clan", two characters are presented in the mode of a dialogue, although, it is the voice of the orphan's grandmother that one hears throughout. The orphan must play the role of a listener to the more experienced grandmother. Hence, the technique of silence within the active voice of the old woman is meant to establish this deference. The grandmother's voice constantly reminds us of the presence of a listener. Phrases such as "your mother", "I told your people" and "But she left you" show a special form of dialogue in which voice and silence are dramatically juxtaposed. In the section titled "village elder", it is in the voice of the old man that one perceives the orphan's pensive mood. The old man understands the orphan's dilemma and he proceeds to mediate upon him:

>Wake up, orphan!
>Wake from the null of the cold pain
>In your mutilated taproot;
>Wake, and wade through the mist

---

[27]Okello Oculi, *Orphan*. (Nairobi: East African Publishing House, 1968): 8. All subsequent page references are made to this edition and appear in the text.

> Over your eyes. Be a man. (p. 35)

This is one of the many moments of dramatic interplay between the orphan and the various individuals in the text. Here, the metaphors of "mutilated taproot" and "the mist over [the] eyes" are used to express the orphan's disconnected self.

One finds a different performance mode in the poetry of the much younger Ugandan poet, Susan Kiguli. In her "The African Saga", title poem of her new poetry collection, the African political saga is cast in a performance mode. Kiguli constructs this poem by building a performance structure into the text. The drums and the ragged chorus occur as still images in the written text but they easily translate into active agents in a dramatic reading or life performance of "The African Saga". This is to say that the performance mode, which she incorporates is easily retrievable in a dramatic reading in which the actions of the text are mimed and the listeners become a participatory audience. The lines of the poem reveal these performance potentials:

> The ballot boxes set in place
> The curtain draws back
> To thunderous throbbing drums.
> The ragged but indomitable chorus
> Stands itself lame
> To cast the vote...
>
> The antagonist struts out
> Like a cock at dawn...
> He shoots venomous arrows
> Into the expectant audience...
> All the parted lips
> Are stuffed with live charcoal
> Red hot winking charcoal!
> Usually one peasant gulping fire
> Chokes on it in hilarious laughter,
> Ha ha, some farce.[28]

The use of the oral narrative mode appears to be the area in which Oculi maintains the strongest tie with p'Bitek. Like p'Bitek, Oculi uses this voice as a critical apprehension of the issue of the African cultural experience. Again, like p'Bitek, the voice we hear in Oculi's *Orphan* is that of a protesting woman. In the section titled "woman whose husband is of Okello's clan", the speaker

---

[28]Susan Kiguli, *The African Saga*. (Kampala: Femrite Publications, 1998): 12.

demonstrates her opposition to the new culture that alienates the African elites from their own people:

> When Okello joins the clan
> of "yes, no" people he will
> Say he is going to the Office
> On my funeral day.
> Where will he find the hands to carry
> My dirty wrinkled village body
> To the grave?
> Where would be the soap, the dettol
> To wash off my smell from his suit,
> And the polish to cleanse off the
> Grave soil from his "Made
> In Italy" shoes?
> If he came to my funeral
> Where would the village people
> Find chai and coffee
> And cook Lunch, and Dinner and Break hunger
> For his prostitute Secretary (p. 45)

The woman does not lament a culture being eroded, she rather is concerned with the position of the African elites who in her opinion are uprooted individuals. She defines their alienation from the perspectives of their adopted names and religion. For the speaker, birth names

> ... are the record of the pulse
> Of our hearts at the shrine of birth
> When the navel is cut and the nipple's
> Yearn for sucking is answered! (p. 46)

The questionable morality of the new religion calls the attention of the speaker who asks rhetorically:

> When a young girl leaves
> Singing love songs
> On the grinding stone
> To sing grave songs of strange
> People of strange tongues,
> And takes her breasts to ripen in
> The catechism chorus rituals,
> And reports of the scratch of rough beards
> Of sacrifice on her shea butter smooth
> Cheeks,
> Am I blind to the wizardry of the crucified?
> Witch doctor? (p. 50)

For this speaker, personal experience becomes the means of validating the essence or values of a culture. So, she takes the purity of her own womanhood as a reflection of the sanity in traditional life. Fertility imagery is used here to evoke the idea of a culture that tends life:

> The hills of my womb have not been denuded
> By the white man's pills; the medicines of
> Death have not corroded my womb; my womb
> Has never been a coffin, never been a grave for
> A baby from the medicines of civilization!
> My womb is pure: I have never been a walking
> Carrier of death; a giggling gas chamber of
> Anyone's baby...
> The fertility of my womb shall never
> Enrich dustbins and public utilities
> With abortions done for fashion (p. 68)

On the other hand, the new urban culture produces the ruined maid, the type we find in Mapanje's "Messages". Here again, the speaker describes the sanity of her womanhood in subdued sexual images:

> My cow hoof, my drainage trench,
> My moon trail,
> The passage of what I am, and
> The route of my sanity,
> This stamp of my womanhood is no interest-laden
> Loan from the Good Spirit.
> Who has ever sold a mouth to a tooth brush seller? (p. 69)

The speaker's self pride contrasts with the ruined maid personality which she associates with "the woman of town" (p. 69) who inhabits "the place of the devil" (p. 69) and "celebrates the latest abortion, with the/ Alcohol of machines from chemists" (p. 69). Oculi's image of the orphan is evidently more complex than it appears in the text. By being disconnected from their cultural roots, the various characters revealed to us through the voice are cultural orphans.

The Orphan Complex

The orphan image in Oculi's book embodies various levels of disconnection. The more obvious level is the image of the motherless child who suffers the agony of a disconnection from the mother figure. Oculi develops the orphan motif around the character of Okello, the orphan boy. He adopts the dirge form to express the orphan's laments. One notices the dirge tone from the first few lines of *Orphan*. In "Okello the orphan", the orphan's voice is a reflection on personal loss: "The woman whose breasts I sucked/Is gone to the worms" (p. 11). These lines are significant because they bear the contrasting images of life and death, which define the sense and mood of the entire collection. A woman's breasts represent life source. It is therefore imperative that the child connects the mother figure. Of course, the image of worms evokes the awesomeness of death and the speaker is drawn back into a sudden realization of the fact of his disconnection. The disconnected child is a prey in the complex external world:

> The woman whose tender care,
> Like the termites that come when the hens
> Have wiped their beaks for the day,
> I missed,
> Left me to the whims of kites's appetites
> While she eloped with the Wild Cat.
> Deaf to my screams of goodbye unintended,
> She left me to the cuddle of loneliness. (p. 12)

Oculi employs the oral style in which the contrasting states of life and death are built into the structure of the dirge. Life is imaged as a ceremony of passage in which we are presented with a woman who pushes a child through the birth-trough:

> When her sinews twanged and her
> Trunk repulsed
> And she defied the shame of dung forgotten out
> In her sweat bath
> Under insults of terrored midnight nerves
> And clang yells of tingling metals
> To pull her out of labour's depths
> And scream me into existence (p. 12)

The orphan goes back in time, making a self-portrait as a newborn being celebrated "in the hut of birth" (p. 12) by "the chatter of women in joy" (p. 12). His birth is a symbol of the renewal of the link with the ancestors:

> "He is one of us - from the Ancestors -
> The Ancestors have come to us again -
> Call him Okello - he told the twins
> To come and allow his turn too -
> Okello, we offer you these hands
> When we are still around - come -
> Okello, suck your mother - grow up to bury us!" (p. 13)

However, the atmosphere of celebration turns into mourning as the orphan tells us about his mother's death:

> I thought my mother would show me to the Path

> And shake off the first dews
> And pull off the thorns fond of my delicate
> Uncertain feet,
> But she left me to stumble on stubble
> And scream tears dry off my eyes
> Along the Path, alone!
> Away with the Wild Cat
> She left my screams to frighten nibbling
> Rats under bushes
> And cork ears of grazing cows,
> Cows mixing waves of appetite and jolts. (p. 14)

The narrator (the orphan) employs images that invoke the idea of an innocent child who loses his unity with the mother figure. Death is imaged as a mystery, which is far beyond what the orphan child could reasonably comprehend. So, he imagines death only in relation to the image of termites, which are hurried "to fires invading the grip of peaceful darkness" (p. 14) in a collective death "in the cooking pot of trappers" (p. 14). His mother's death is understood only in the practical sense of the absence of someone who could respond to "the echoes of the questions/ in [his] scream" (p. 14) and the curiosity of the innocent child "deep beneath the embracing/stars in [his] virgin eyes" (p. 11). Within the traditional setting that Oculi opens to us, the orphan is a symbol of collective nurture. In this case, the whole village is involved in mediating upon him. In "village elder" for instance, such mediation occurs through an old man who commits his experience to the re-habilitation of the orphan's fragmented self. The old man is the symbol of experience and he inspires the orphan with words from folk wisdom:

> Orphan boy, you must learn to expect little
> From the generosity of the world,
> To grapple alone with the top of the earth,
> As the baby must will to walk
> And teach its wobbly feet the harsh
> Truth of hunters,
> And of young courtiters and men
> Whose wives other men do not
> Knock on the grass
> To pay the food the women have begged;
> That the world laughs
> At idle wishers that dread pain
> To earn a desired good. (p. 29)

The old man's rhetorical device is one in which inspiring words are structured as traditional wits. We hear the voice of the sage engaging the orphan directly: "My son, tragedy is not a marriage feast/To which people flock in broad daylight" (p. 37). For the old man, life is "[t]wisted humour" (p. 36) with its antithesis of "Chasms and walls of silence" and "turns of warm gayness" (p. 38). The process of growing up involves the recognition of this complexity and again, the old man is the figure from whom the disconnected orphan must learn the act of dealing with this complexity. The oral medium of transmitting this equally involves certain pattern of images. Such a pattern reflects in Ocul's use of the metaphor of hunting to express the physical and psychic components of initiation into manhood:

> Wake to stand the echo
> And cold vibrations in your bowels
> When the roar of the wounded lion thunders
> And quakes all around;
> Face the dark eyes of ultimate loneliness
> At the surge of a lion's angry mass
> In the *arum* hunt wilderness:
> Ridiculing, dissolving man's being
> Under the advancing darkness of its upright
> Charge behind its aimed paw
> And challenged mountain rage. (p. 36)

The central image here is *arum*, which the poet describes as "a big communal hunt across the wilderness" (p. 102). Thus, to draw the orphan into *arum* is to help him discover his manhood and locate him within a communal life far from the brooding aloneness, which the orphan complex imposes on him.

Apart from Okello, Oculi uses another point of view in his exploration of the orphan motif. This is the voice described by the poet as "Okello's milk sister". This character is obviously less developed than most of the voices but her story helps to amplify the dirge tone in the text. Like Okello her brother, she reflects on the finality of death and the severance of the link between mother and child. This voice expresses personal grief and the futility of life through an extended metaphor in which her dead mother is represented as the woman who is

> Gone out without a return
> Before the fire she lit in the cooking place
> Had caught the wood and the flames,
> Had began to sing and scowl,
> Feeling ripe and ready for the challenge
> Of performing the pregnancy rites
> Of the cooking pot. (p. 89)

Without a mother to guide her, the orphan girl is left to fantasize in "clouds of girlhood" (p. 92), the bucolic world in which a girl acts out her maiden roles under the watchful eyes of the proud mother of her invention:

> Without a mother to love you,
> To pretend disgust in the sweet hollow ways
> Of a proud woman in mocking
> At her loved one;
> To caringly mock as your groping voice
> With coy courage of venturesome youth
> Rises to sing in melody with the hums
> Of the grinding stone and the chorus
> Of laughing millet grains;
> To steal looks at your unripe neck-breaking
> And your waist and breast wriggling
> And then palm down and away
> Her joy's smiles;
> To reveal her prides for herself in you
> Through her loud complaints about
> Many nothings. (p. 91)

Landscape, Images and Symbols

Landscape plays an important role in shaping Oculi's creativity and vision. The grassland setting and the pastoral tradition that is built on it are sources of images, which demonstrate a specific form of experience. Oculi describes himself as a product of the pastoral tradition and for him the most compelling image or vision of life could be drawn from simply watching the cattle grazing on the field. According to him, one is easily able to appreciate life from new perspectives by reflecting on such image:

> One of the images I remember very well ... When the cattle are moving under the trees you hear this rustle of dry leaves as the cows rush from one place to the other looking for what to eat. One thing that comes out is that the energy life puts into the search for continued survival is incredible - these animals insisting on recovering the source of life. At the same time, life is trampling on what has already lost its own living. The leaves are dead and the cattle don't seem to notice that. I always indicate the paradox of one life being unaware of death in the other. Sometimes, life is at the expense of another life.[29]

Of course it is easy to draw this kind of insight, given the tie that exists between Man and animal within pastoral tradition. The various figures in *Orphan* communicate their feelings through animal referents. For instance, in

---

[29]Charles Bodunde, "Interview with Okello Oculi".

placing material tradition in proper perspective, Okello's maternal grandmother refers to bride price in terms of cow heads: "You see - your mother was married- /The cows came from this house" (p. 17). The cow symbol reflects the ways in which the pastoral community is constituted. Beyond being a bride price, the cow is the symbol of the blood link between families and communities. Already, Okello the orphan is a product of this linkage. His mother's death brings him back to his family origin, the origin of the cows of his mother's dowry. The grandmother refers to the cow symbol again to reassure Okello that he has a right in his father's household. There is also a spiritual dimension to this symbol and it reflects in the grandmother's voice. Okello is the link between his dead mother and the household. His task is to tend the cattle in his uncle's kraal. By tending the kraal, he is gradually preparing a home, the tradition of continuity that the cow symbol reflects. This continuity is suggested in the grandmother's placatory remark:

> But she left you,
> To speak for her and plead with
> The cows in your uncles' kraal to suckle their
> Calves and release the milk in their udders.
> You will mend the crack in the walls
> And quieten the protest in my wrinkled flaps,
> And I can sleep again.
> You are of us, my intestines, my husband! (p. 18)

Thus, cattle stand as the status symbol and the means of negotiating social and cultural expectations. As Oculi puts it, "the man without cows for a wife" (p. 31) is always the object of ridicule :

> Women whose compounds are blessed
> With a kraal
> Say his walk is clumsy
> Like the snake in the newly
> Ploughed field,
> His teeth project out of his
> Mouth like a warthog's
> And he crawls in walking as
> If yaws fill between his buttocks.
> They insult him that his
> Body is cold with the shadow
> Spirits of dead wizards who were
> His uncles,
> And that his skin is taut and dry
> As if the back side of a penis bore him!

57

Again, in Okello's sister's narrative, the speaker fantasizes about nuptial ceremony. In her dream world, cows are the central symbol and she uses visual and sound images to convey the ways in which these animals set the atmosphere in a bridal ceremony:

>Afraid of the rumble of the thunder
>Provoking rumbles of hooves,
>Of hooves for my dowry,
>Excited hooves surging and charging towards
>The kraal of my father,
>Cows running, and jogging and kicking out
>In fits and mocks and in a melee of excitement
>From the smell of the imminent rains;
>Cows and goats and sheep
>Waving horns and dangling udders,
>Heralds coming on and on
>Bringing home the message of my mother's arrogant
>Triumph;
>Dancing and kicking up dust and
>Dancing the fulfillment dance
>Amid bellowing and mooing
>Proud *ijira* calls, and beating up *kaluulu*
>To my mother's birth of a daughter. (pp. 93-94)

The cow symbol also embodies the family pride. Okello's "milk sister" is the symbol of the repair of the homestead. In a passionate manner, she renders the vision of a woman who is conscious of her roles as wife and sister and the need to help build a new life, a new homestead:

>I shall bring the cows home
>Dowry cows and goats and sheep,
>To buy estates for a place in the open sun
>For Okello's pride.
>I shall drink the growls of a husband, all,
>Without a drop of a grumble
>Breathe in,
>Latrine odours oozing out of a drunken husband,
>Of my man decomposed in sodden abandon on me;
>I shall roast cowhide for our meal of the night
>With a husband who has no arms,
>Do all,
>Suffer all with the calm silence of a sheep
>And patient care of a cobweb spider,
>To bring the torch of freedom into the darkness
>In Okello's boy-hut. (p. 95)

In *Orphan*, there is a variety of image-making which is connected to the pastoral imagery and vision found in Oculi's quoted remark about cattle grazing in the field. In at least three sections of *Orphan*, Oculi relates the cow and grass imagery to explore human attitude. The cow may eat as much grass as it wants but in the section titled "Okello's stepmother", we are reminded that "The grass in the front thatch of the hut/Is sacred" (p. 80). This image recurs in "a man" where the speaker talks of "The inedible grasses around the hut" (p. 86). Unlike the grass around the hut, the distant grass is food for the cattle, not a taboo. This pastoral mythology connects the existent psycho-cultural archetype, which manifests itself in what one may simply describe as the sacrifice of otherness. In a slightly different way, the cow symbol is used as a technique in exploring the mystery of death in the series titled "Okello's mother's uncle". Here, the speaker dialogues with Okello on the subject of death. To create sense out of the dialogue, the speaker sets the paradox of the pests (agent of death) which "leaves behind/ The cows with the dry udders in the kraal" (p. 20) against the image of "Death's victory tug" (p. 20) at a woman with milk. Of course, the speaker uses the line, "The cows with the dry udders" to symbolize old women.

Oculi transfers certain symbols and aesthetic modes in oral poetry in order to convey specific aspects of reality. Again, like p'Bitek, Oculi uses the spear and the horn as symbols, which reflect levels of human aspiration. The spear euphemistically refers to a man's sexual power. Oculi's handling of this symbol relates to the sense in which Pieter Fourie uses it in *Shaka* to express the passionate love between Shaka and Pampata, his wife. Here, the spear symbol is the medium for articulating sexual union:

> Shaka will mount his finest heifer and from the copper shaft of
> his spear shoot white like stars a thousand tiny assegais into the
> dark womb between her thighs.[30]

In "village elder", the old man employs the spear as a symbol of a man's desire for physical strength. In a subtle manner, the man extends this symbol to express sexual thrust. The two meanings are interlinked in a deft manoeuvre of images:

> Walk to a spear
> And learn the message of facing, alone,
> The twang of its stem and the silent power
> In its blade;
> Rise to face isolation's challenge
> In the teasing charge of a girl's beckoning

---

[30]Pieter Fourie, *Shaka*. (Cape Town: Longmans Penguin, 1976): 70.

> Breasts, swinging in the "get fixed" dance
> In moonlight;
> Ripe breasts of youth
> Daring you to her loving body
> Boiling and steaming opiums of passion
> From rhythmic tremors,
> Melting and rippling perfumed motions
> With and towards the depth
> Of the heave and talk of drums in melodious
> Self rendering;
> Drums yearning to pour out all
> In a final act of self-fulfillment.(p. 35)

Dance is also used as a symbol, which builds on the sexual motif. The "get fixed" dance is the symbol of sexual embrace, an act which also signifies a certain level of social consciousness and maturity. Symbolically, the spear is a man's response to the woman

> Dancing to dissolve herself
> In the honey of rhythmic intoxication,
> Vibrating, on and on, to annihilate her
> Being in the ether of the orgasm at
> The fusion ground of melody and the spirit
> In her yearning for the depths of realization.
> Challenging all being around her
> With her fire,
> Knowing even the heavens will not exhaust
> Her power;
> Calling on the skies and the bowels of the
> Forests
> To behold the ripples of the waves
> In her liquid buttocks, melting
> With the advancing provocation of drum waves
> Bashing the shores of her body in moonlight
> Dance. (pp. 35-36)

Spear, horn and drum are also part of the symbol fields of the female voices in *Orphan*. For instance, the female figure in "Okello's stepmother" proclaims the pride of her Akwali dance team and their youthful excitement through "succulent horns" (p. 79) and "the intoxicating spine-dissolving/...bellow of drums" (p. 79). This speaker also weaves the spear symbol into a satire against the city *femme fatale* who "trap from other women the power/of their young spears" (p. 75). Also, the spear becomes the revealing symbol in "village gossip" where the female speaker stirs a witch-hunt in a vituperative onslaught:

> That woman who hides the faeces of others'

>Children among her vegetables
>And has trapped the fertility of many women
>In her dark charcoal eyes,
>And tied up the power of the spear of many
>Young men with herbs from her wizard mother;
>That woman who thinks she will
>Never laugh the whiteness of her
>Teeth to the worms in the soil,
>Killed your mother! (p. 24)

There is a different interpretation of the orphan phenomenon especially when one relates *Orphan* to *Malak*, Oculi's other book of poetry. The orphan image includes the broader interpretation of the African historical experience. For Oculi, the orphan concept embodies a symbolic connection between the orphan status and Africa, which has lost a link with its own essence and has become fragmented. The process of being orphaned is also exemplified in Africa's colonial experience, which Oculi says, amounts to "the defeat of a people."[31] With this defeat, Oculi further argues, "the sense of mourning is even greater [and] it is easy to come up with the concept of orphan. Here were an orphan people."[32] Oculi also associates genocidal politics in Africa with the orphan complex arguing that one cannot build a nation by making people orphans."[33] In *Malak*, Oculi's image of the African landscape and experience connects the orphan syndrome. Here, the picture is a landscape disconnected from its peoples:

>I look East of here
>and I see graveyards of railway and timber companies
>and cotton planters' bones
>spread across brown soils of Central African Republic
>and Gabon
>and Kongo;
>graveyards of men for whom no graves were dug
>and no parliamentary questions asked;
>men from Gambia, Senegal
>from Upper Volta and from Cameroon too,
>dragged from their wives and mothers poorly left behind,
>to dig and cut History and clothe *civilization*.[11]

---

[31] Charles Bodunde, "Interview with Okello Oculi".
[32] ibid.
[33] ibid.
[11] Okello Oculi, *Malak*. (Nairobi: East African Publishing House, 1976): 15. All subsequent page references are made to this edition and appear in the text.

> The problem is even more compounded as the people themselves are torn apart by genocide:
>
> My ears hear a great loneliness
> for here they have been depopulating one another.
> Too many have left:
> men dying
> and the land expanding all around those still holding on,
> and with each man, each child, a seed dies.
> Relatives go;
> languages disappear to be heard only in the branches
> of trees on a windy night;
> neighbours cannot be counted on anymore to come
> and share a meal or name a new-born baby
> for they too left this solitude unaccompanied. (p. 15)

However, in the concluding lines of Oculi's *Malak*, there is the vision of a new Africa, mediated upon (like Okello) and showing signs of a break from the orphan complex of hopelessness to "a whisper in the clouds/urging to be born" to make "new Niles and Nigers and Kongos" (p. 63).

VI. KOFI ANYIDOHO AND THE EWE FUNERAL DIRGE

The Ewe funeral dirge is the most important influence on Kofi Anyidoho's poetry. With a mother who rose to the position of the leader of the town's dirge group, Anyidoho experienced a first hand contact with a unique aesthetic form that was to determine the shape and direction of his poetry. He acknowledges his debt to the Ewe dirge and offers a description of its theme and tone:

> Some of my poems are very closely modeled on the Ewe traditional poetry, particularly on the dirge tradition ... In terms of the impulse, the dirge impulse for the Ewes goes beyond the fact of death as the end to everything: there is always a certain projection beyond death, that's why there is that combination of a real sadness with a touch of optimism, the ability to look beyond the present circumstances of sorrow.[1]

A much earlier influence of the Ewe dirge shows in the works of Kofi Awoonor, another Ghanaian poet. Awoonor provides useful insights into the understanding of the nature of the Ewe funeral dirge in his poetry and also in a PhD dissertation where he defines the genre in terms of context of performance, purpose and performance techniques:

> Dirge, in the broadest sense...is the lament for the dead. The elaborate African funeral, from the wailing and ululation through the first burial and second or final burial, provides occasion for poetry. This type may be described as philosophical, seeking the meaning and purpose of life, and has an expected tone of solemnity and sorrow.[2]

In approaching Anyidoho's transfer of the dirge, a textual analysis is adopted and for this purpose, one depends on the various poems in *A Harvest of Our Dreams*. One must state generally that in the transposition of the Ewe dirge, repetition is the most conspicuous technique which reflects in this collection. Speaking of the ways in which repetition manifests itself within the Ewe dirge, Awoonor contends that the dominant patterns we are likely to encounter are "repetition of lines, or of large segments, repetition of imagery and of sound" and that the specific function of the form is to "enhance the chorality of the lament."[3] Harold Scheub describes the function of repetition in image-making

---

[1] Jane Wilkinson, *Talking with African Writers: Interviews*. (London: James Currey, 1992): 9.

[2] Kofi Awoonor, *A Study of the Influences of Oral Literature on the Contemporary Literature of Africa*. (State University of New York at Stony Brook, PhD dissertation, 1972): 23.

[3] ibid: 24.

and in the shaping of aesthetic relations between the oral artist and the audience in the context of a live performance:

> If a key emotion evoking device in a narrative is the image, the major shaping tool is repetition, the patterning of various kinds that includes anticipation and predictability as essential aesthetic adjuncts. Patterning of image, moreover, continues to elicit emotions even as it shapes and clarifies that response. The artist manipulates images, the emotionally experienced activities of diverse characters projected by means of words and the body, to establish the contours of form. The audience is, in a sense, both spectator and participant; it is a part of the raw material of the performance.[4]

Most often, repetition in Anyidoho's poetry comes in the form of parallelism, a related form, which helps to intensify the atmosphere of lament or grief. Also, Anyidoho uses the repetition of the key images of seed, harvest and ghost to create a tonal pattern and a unity of theme, which show the way in which the poems in the collection are organized. Thus, one recognizes a pattern of linkages among the poems and then, the fact that they are integrated into a single structure.

Harvests, Dreams and Hope

Meanings in Anyidoho's harvest imagery are of course shaped by the dirge genre. Anyidoho stretches this genre to accommodate shades of meanings. What he does in "A Harvest of our Dreams", the title poem, is to create a complex of contrasting poetic figures and tones to expand the harvest imagery. One finds image patterns showing harvests becoming losses and then of people struggling against defeat. The lost harvest theme is most evident in the metaphor of the honeybee that collects "fragrance from dreaming waterlilies/from lonely desert blooms"[5], only to be lost to another gatherer who "came with plans/all for his own desires" (p. 6) and set the hive on fire. This imagery accommodates all forms of interpretations concerning the problems of exploitation and abuse that dominate the African historical experience. Anyidoho emphasizes the agony of lost harvests and dreams in repeated lines:

> We will hum a dirge for a burden of these winds ...
> And harvests go ungathered in our time ...
> We will hum a dirge for a burden of these winds ...
> And harvests go ungathered in our time. (pp. 6-7)

---

[4] Harold Scheub, *The Tongue is Fire: South African Storytellers and Apartheid.* (Madison: The University of Wisconsin Press, 1996): 150-151.

[5] Kofi Anyidoho, *A Harvest of Our Dreams.* (London: Heinemann, 1984): 6. All subsequent page references are made to this edition and appear in the text.

In creating the image of hope, the poet reinterprets harvest as a product of the soul. Hope and expectations show in the image of the "unfinished harvests of our soul" (p. 7) that erect "stakes/across our new rainbows... in seasons of harvest dance" (p. 6). Anyidoho uses the harvest image to represent the vision of hope rather than material objects. In "Renegade", for instance, he employs the images of the carrion birds and the dove to reflect on the temporal nature of material objects ("the feast of rot" p. 52) and the re-creative capacity that inhere in visioning. For Anyidoho, the crows of this world may peck at the eyes of the man whose harvest is vision, "but the harvest of his dreams/will not belong to the vampire." (p. 52)

The Ewe dirge celebrates the ancestors as sacred and death is regarded as a journey, a form of union with the spirit being. Images such as the homestead, the orphan and carrion birds like the vulture and crow are common icons in the aesthetic field of the dirge singer. A quick example is Anyidoho's association of the vulture with death in the poem titled "Renegade". In this poem, death is expressed in the image of vultures which "smell rumours of blood flowing in open fields" (p. 52) from their "hideouts in carnage grooves" (p. 52). In "My Last Testimony", the death of a dancer becomes an occasion for general grief. Death is captured euphemistically as taking "the way of flesh" (p. 58) and dancing "on heels in a backwards/loop into the narrow termite home" (p. 58). Death and sorrow are also imaged as dreams "placed among the thorns" and "are still unhatched" (p. 59).

Anyidoho constructs patterns of repetition in which lines and images (the leopard and the panther) are reordered to capture a community broken down into orphan clan by the new predatory culture:

> Whatever befalls the panther in the jungle
> The leopard would not forget about the hunt...
> Whatever befalls the leopard in his ambush
> The panther could not betray the spirit of the hunt...
> Whatever befalls the panther in the desert
> The leopard would not forget the jungle war... (pp. 58-59)

In "Back to Memory", the image of "chains of life" (p. 61) reveals a cycle of life and death. This experience is accentuated by the antithesis in the voice that speaks of "fields littered with corpses of dreams" (p. 61) and "dreams...trapped by long shadows of life" (p. 62). The counterpoints of life and death are also emphasized through repetition and line manipulation:

> running away from memory
> searching for reasons to die...
> long-before the flash of lightning

>   smote down hellgate, letting loose
>   the thousand fiends that today
>   you pursue across deserts and battlefields
>   sending your mind
>   running away from memory
>   searching for reasons to die...
>   and you will mount the clouds
>   to the house of storms where
>   guardian demons relieve the mind
>   of its useless burden of death...
>   They will send you back to memory
>   Make you rich with reasons not to die. (pp. 61-62)

In "Festival of Hopes", Anyidoho employs objects and time elements as symbols to express a people's struggle to conquer their fears and sorrow. Here, one finds symbolic objects like the "big brown calabash, container of the clan's tear...[and] public tears", the "gourd of toils" and "the hearth" where the flames engulf "the pot of blood". These objects, together with time elements patterned as "3rd cock crow", "Noon" and "Dusk" symbolize a people's passage from collective sorrow to a celebration of life. The poem initially reflects a community crushed into silence by grief and tears:

>   Then the Clan appeared.
>   Around the grounds they threw a ring,
>   their jaws still locked in a 7-day communion with Silence.
>   One by one,
>   Man by man
>   they stepped into the ring, bowed.
>   Publicly, silently, they shed their private fears
>   draining their secret cares
>   into that big brown calabash, container of the Clan's tears. (p. 88)

The structure of the poem reflects a movement from grief to hope and the turning point emerges in the "Dusk" section where the poet shifts to the image of chants breaking through silence, "stirring frozen heartbeats of older worlds" (p. 89) flying fast across "closed chapters of life" (p. 90). The symbols of light and cloud are also significant in this sense. We hear of the "clap of clouds" (p. 90) at dusk and "a shaft of light" (p. 95) which break out from the sky and set "the pile of [dead] wood into fire":

>   A clap of clouds, a shaft of light
>   and distraught meteor struck the pile of wood,
>   inflaming the hearth, the flames engulfing the pot of blood,
>   flooding the festive grounds with a glory
>   made hoary by crazed shadows of dazed clansmen
>   each wrestling with his mortal self in

> a jubilant desperation to evoke the second self.
> The flames made a triple leap and grabbed
> the gourd of sweat and calabash of tears.
> Excitement seized an old clansman- he tossed
> himself above the flames and landed neat
> in the pot of boiling blood. (p. 90)

In "Mythmaker", Anyidoho emphasizes the themes of loss and grief using the funeral dirge tone and the device of repetition. The sense of loss is tempered with optimism for absence is interpreted as a temporary departure into "school rooms where the world in book/distils day dreams into visions" burning "memorials of the past/in bonfires of the soul" (p. 2). The poem's dedication sets a sombre tone by alluding to incidents of political crisis and of lives lost in an uprising against a leadership captured by the poet in the image of panther. In a way, the poem is politically overt for the poet attempts to grapple with the political scenario of Ghana in the late 70s. In this regard, the panther becomes an appropriate image for a military leadership that preys on the people. The panther image appears quite popular among African poets especially in relation to their portrait of political oppression. We have already mentioned this image in relation to Okigbo's political dirge, "Elegy for slit-drum" which expresses the Nigerian predatory politics of the 60s in which the military and the politicians turn the civil population into victims.[6]

Anyidoho's "Mythmaker" reflects a society in need of committed leaders whose task is to mediate political life by humanizing it in such a way as to create a condition for the renewal of hope. For the poet, new hope should spring out of the people's sacrifice. One aspect of this is the poet's allusion to the mental and physical strains, which the Ghanaian youth must endure to trap that knowledge which is most vital for securing the future. Sacrifice is captured in the image of a harsh weather and we hear the poet speaking of youth plucking "poison kisses from laurels" which bloom "with rage in mid-winter" (p. 2). Here, journey is taken as a form of death, a kind of passage into a new consciousness or knowledge. Home, to the returning new elites is a place of death and decay:

> But they will sign to see how for six seasons
> our mothers fed on new dirges
> our common *kenkey* grown so lean
> we needed a decree to insure her health
> our scholars, deployed from campuses
> into ghost communal farms,
> walked the streets at dawn like zombies

---

[6] Christopher Okigbo, *Labyrinths*. (London: Heinemann, 1971): 68.

> peddling posters proclaiming final obsequies
> for the revolution that went astray.
> They will be hit by stray bullets
> They will be clubbed to death in dark corners
> And we will hear of brass band processions
> congregating at our Castle of despair
> celebrating the victory of our death. (p. 3)

Knowledge is captured in "Mythmaker" as the metaphor for life. It incarnates the essential forces of renewal making the dead the living, exiles as returnees and funeral dirges as celebration of life:

> Some day they will be home
> for final rites for the late renegades.
> Their garlands will pass for wreaths.
> And yet somehow they won't be sad or mad.
> They will turn and return to a bereaved home
> and still they won't be mad or sad.
> Though our memory of life now boils
> into vapours, the old melody of hope
> still clings to tenderness of hearts
> locked in caves of stubborn minds. (p. 3)

Repetition is used in the poem to emphasize the dirge element and in a unique way, it also indicates the poet's vision of hope. As is typical of Anyidoho, grief is tempered with the counter-tone of optimism and hence, the joy of homecoming becomes a welcome alternative to the sadness in parting:

> The children are away
> The children are away
> The children
> These children are
> away. (p. 3)

And in the same stream the poet says optimistically:

> The children will be home
> The children will be home
> The children
> Those children will
>   be home
>   someday. (p. 3)

Images of decay and regeneration and the tones of grief and hope run through the lines of *A Harvest of our Dreams*. In "Seedtime", Anyidoho examines the political history of Ghana. Nkrumah's lost revolution is expressed in the metaphor of lost harvests. These losses are „the thoughts that bring the tears/upon the harvest of our dreams" (p. 4). Here again, grief is relieved by hope, which is beyond the current "gift of thunder" (p. 4) and the rainstorm that destroys the vision laid "across the backyard of the skies" (p. 5). The poet refers to the people's growing determination to live and reconstruct their thoughts "into new cobwebs of life" (p. 4) so that the "predator birds" (p. 5) that exploit them politically "shall have to prey upon their own anger their own nightmares" (p. 5). The poet's hope is also beyond mere dreams because what he anticipates is a leader who genuinely represents the people's vision and could therefore initiate a collective proclamation:

> There is no curse on us
> There is no curse on us...
> We will not die the death of dreams
> We will not die the cruel death of dreams (p. 5)

Beyond Lament: The Metaphor of Rebirth

The series of poems under "Akofa" (part two) are rendered as pieces of performance. This style accommodates the conversational mode and the choral form, which situates the dirge genre in its natural performance context. Talking about performance aesthetic as a way of sustaining orality in written text, Anyidoho argues that the current experience has gone beyond mere theoretical statement. He states that many of his published poems are conceived within the tradition of a total art, which incorporates oral forms:

> I took published poems of mine, working with the resident theatre company of the University of Ghana and did a full scale dramatization. We took the poem and treated them like a script for a play. We worked with the concept of what we described as a total art (involving music, dance), everything coming together. When it first came on at the Drama Studio in Accra, the greatest testimony was from a daughter of our colleague, Atukwei Okai, a seven-year old girl who sat in the audience watching the performance. Her father reported to me that when it was over [the performance] and people started clapping, she made a comment in Gaa and repeated it about three times: *a me bomode* meaning, these people have done well. The performance was in English. She didn't probably understand everything but she was clearly impressed ... That particular production was followed by several others by me and my colleagues. So, a tradition of poetry dramatization emerged.[7]

Anyidoho sees the "re-presentation of written poetry through the multiple media of African performance tradition" as a development that "holds great potential for overcoming the communication gap that has forced the poet, as a

---

[7] Charles Bodunde, "Interview with Kofi Anyidoho". *Tape Recording* 26th March, 1999, Fez, Morocco.

writer, into an often celebrated but clearly marginalized position as a contemporary artist."[8]

The performance mode is specifically employed in composing "Fertility", a poem in which repetition and the choral medium are deployed to develop the themes of absence and agony. In a note to the poem, Anyidoho informs us: "in public performance the opening line should be repeated by the audience throughout the entire poem" (p. 19). The opening line reads: "come back home Agbenoxevi come back home" (p. 19). Ezenwa Ohaeto interprets the line as the signature of dirge. His argument is that

> The opening poem, „Fertility Game", is a lament in the true Ewe dirge tradition as the persona insists with a refrain, „come back home Agbenoxevi come back home" ... The voice of Agbenoxevi is expected to „rise deep across the years" which highlights the trope of sadness, for it could be said to be a „field" where there was tremendous suffering and an image of the terrible tribulations of the people. However, the ideas that those „who died" would „live again" or that those who die „wake up with seeds of life sprouting from their graves" portray the poet's concept in the utilization of the Ewe dirge tradition to comment on present reality and generate hope.[9]

There is no doubt about the dirge tone in the repeated line and the general climate of hope in Anyidoho's "Fertility". However, the line in question certainly has a wider implication especially when it is perceived in the context of cultural vision and practice. The appeal to Agbenoxevi is to reintegrate him into community life symbolized in "the wrestling duel of song and dance" (p. 19) in which "maidens will sharpen their tongues and carve praise images of dream lovers..." (p. 19). In this sense, Anyidoho's "Fertility" is linked with Osundare's „Akintunde come Home" and Mapanje's "Messages" where the individual voices express the need to reintegrate those who are lost to the community. The central symbol of the poem is love and the poet reflects its character through a speaker who describes a woman's love as a man's vision into life's regenerative essences manifesting in "deserts and pain fields" (p. 20) where people "died the death of droughts and of wars" (p. 20) and then "lived again... with seeds of life sprouting from their graves" (p. 20). The woman's sexual desire is hidden in the images of restrained passion held "against storms against thunder and the haunting smiles of gods" (p. 20). It is clear that the woman's call is for sexual union and because she represents the values of her

---

[8] Kofi Anyidoho, „Poetry as Dramatic Performance: The Ghanaian Experience". *Research in African Literature* 22, 2 (Summer 1991): 42.

[9] Ezenwa-Ohaeto, "Survival Strategies and the New Life of Orality in Nigerian and Ghanaian Poetry: Osundare's *Waiting Laughters* and Anyidoho's *Earthchild*". *Research in African Literature*. 22, 27 (Summer 1996): 76.

culture, the man achieves a reunion with his culture through her. The union is also a social (even sacred) act of renewal of life, which, as the speaker's lament shows, gives her a passage into womanhood:

> Come back home Agbenoxevi come back home
> All my peers now carry big babies on their back.
> Still I carry mine in my heart. Sometimes in my loins...
> Kokui my young sister went away last Moon
> at harvest time. She swallowed a tiny gourd seed
> so now she carries a giant gourd in her belly
> for Senyo our dying Chief's only living son.
> Even Foli my mother's youngest child
> now speaks in the village school he goes
> pinching the bigger girls on their wosowosos. (p. 21)

The paradox of the link between the fact of dying and of being born is most elegantly sustained in "A Song for Silent Fears". This is a birthday song written in a dirge form that incorporates images of joy and sorrow. The juxtaposition of tones is set off in the poet's gift of a smile concealed in a dirge. In the poem, the vision of life bears the imprint of death. For instance, we are confronted with the images of "corpse of a youth" and "stillborn hopes of youth" (p. 81). However, life picks up again after "the slow rhythm of funeral dance" (p. 81). We hear of "a ritual invocation of suspended joys" (p. 81) which "transformed into excited booms" and "harvest joy" and "festive moods/riding low on shoulders of storms" (p. 81). Also, "the new radiance of smiles" (p. 81) after a dirge anticipates "happy screams of infant life" (p. 81). The paradox of life-in-death also manifests in "A Wreath of Tears" where virgins sing the eternal songs that celebrate "faith in death as/gateway to new desires of newer selves".

The ghost image recurs in Anyidoho's *A Harvest of Our Dreams*. Of course, this kind of image is expected in a dirge. Ghosts are portrayed as the dead who occupy the interface between life and death. Thus, in the title poem, ("A Harvest of Our Dream") we encounter a ghost "on guard/ at Memory's door". Anyidoho also weaves the ghost image in the context of dirge into political statements. In "Diviner's Curse", past failures are recalled in the image of the haunting "dance of ghosts" and "the courtyard of ... song" (p. 11). The image is also extended to apportion blame on the older generation that has failed the community by listening to prophets who offer half-truths to take the "communal ritual feasts" (p. 11). The ghost of past failure becomes the symbol of postcrity, which revisits incidents of past guilt at the collective and individual levels. The repetition device in the poem indicates this:

> The children will come pointing questions at

> Us.
> Here I stand mumbling apologies into my beard
> I spend a fortune rehearsing
> the lies we shall have to tell
> to explain our manhood's failure in prime of youth.
> I teach myself to be wily as the tongue
> to move with craft among the knife-throwers
>
> Thus I become a coward
> to the courage of our thoughts
>
> And the children shall come pointing questions at
> Me. (pp. 11-12)

So far, what one finds to be the products of Anyidoho's reinvented dirge are the patterns of imagery he engages to subvert or temper the grey atmosphere of the funeral dirge making the subjects of life and death the dialectical components of the processes of rebirth and continuity. Also, the transfer of the performance materials of the chanted dirge into the space of the written text (in English) is a purposeful aesthetic innovation. As stated earlier, this kind of transfer supplies the aesthetic resources that lend the text its performance potentials especially when, as Anyidoho himself says, there is a growing desire among African poets to experiment with techniques that help "in returning African poetry to its dramatic oral roots".[10]

---

[10] Kofi Anyidoho, "Poetry as Dramatic Performance: The Ghanaian Experience". :48.

VII. EZENWA OHAETO AND THE MASQUERADE VOICE

Romanus Egudu's pioneering work, *African Poetry of the Living Dead* informs much of what we know as the Igbo masquerade poetry. This corpus is underresearched and as Egudu notes, earlier studies focus more on masquerade as theatre, thereby making it appear as if the poetic component is less significant.[34] This poetic type is rooted in the tradition of masquerades called *Nmonwu* among the Igbo people of Nigeria.[35] According to Egudu, masquerades are believed to be the dead returning to the living in spiritual or supernatural form. This form is represented as a mask.[36] As an ancestral spirit, the masquerade symbolizes that link between the dead and the living and is therefore the custodian of the aesthetic and cultural heritage of the people.

Among the Igbo, masquerades are distinguished according to age, gender and functions. As Egudu tells us, there are

> ... elderly male masquerades (who are usually the poet-chanters), adult male masquerades, teenage male masquerades (called *oliba* in some parts of Igboland), old female masquerades (called *nwaebune* in some places), and young female masquerades... These different types of masquerades perform different functions: some are specialized in chanting, producing poetry; some run around pursuing young men and teenage males in a game-situation; old female masquerades go from compound to compound inspecting them for cleanliness and destroying pots and other household utensils as punishment to the women of the homes for their failure to keep them clean; teenage male and young female masquerades entertain people with dancing.[37]

Of these types only the older male masquerades represent the ancestral spirit.[38]

In *The Voice of the Night Masquerade*, Ezenwa Ohaeto alludes to these masquerade types:

> An old masquerade
> Dances with measured steps
> The *ijele* dances with weighty ceremony
> The Mgbedike dances with energetic steps
> The Agaba is not a mask of songs and dance

---

[34] Romanus N. Egudu, *African Poetry of the Living Dead: Igbo Masquerade Poetry*. (Lewiston: The Edwin Mellen Press, 1992): 39.
[35] ibid: 31.
[36] ibid.
[37] ibid: 31-32.
[38] ibid.

> The night masquerade dances
> To the pulse beats of the throbbing night.[39]

In broader terms, Egudu defines the social and cultural connections and functions which underpin masquerade poetry:

> ... the chanters of this poetry, the ancestral masquerades, had experienced human life fully and are now members of the spirit world, so that the past and the present are simultaneously before their gaze [sic]. Their poetry is therefore produced from the vantage point of omniscience whereby the artists are able to speak about life comprehensively, advising the living on socio-political justice and moral rectitude as well as revealing and correcting the secret vices of the mischievous members of the society.[40]

The genre incorporates other aesthetic forms like folktales, proverbs, anecdotes and folksongs to create a communicative body of art which speaks on a wide range of subjects in a direct voice to a live audience. This performance mode is again emphasized by Egudu who argues that each masquerade poem "is addressed to the audience (people present with or accompanying the artist-masquerade) or a member of that audience, it assumes some dramatic quality: it is an art meant for the well-being of the people and is addressed to them directly in the immediate present."[41]

The concern here is to explore the ways in which Ohaeto exploits the aesthetics of the masquerade poetry to comment on contemporary issues. Ohaeto's *The Voice of the Night Masquerade* is significant for this purpose.

Mask and Mediation

The voice of the masquerade is the central symbol in Ohaeto's *The Voice of the Night Masquerade*. For Ohaeto, the existing crisis atmosphere challenges the genius of the artist. He apprehends this situation by engaging the symbol of the mask as a medium for connecting past memories to influence the present and the future. In "A call at dusk", he re-enacts the invocation of the mask, the icon of past memory and wisdom when society stumbles at "the crossroad" (p. 12). The crossroads icon embodies the point of transition where seemingly contradictory elements are connected to create new values. It is in the crossroads arena that "Spirits meet humans/ Water meets the land/the child meets the adult" (p. 12).

---

[39] Ezenwa Ohaeto, *The Voice of the Night Masquerade*. (Ibadan: Kraft Books Ltd., 1996): 63-64. All subsequent page references are made to this edition and appear in the text.
[40] Romanus N. Egudu, *African Poetry of the Living Dead: Igbo Masquerade Poetry: 36*.
[41] Ibid: 37.

The poet recreates the context of masquerade poetry chants in which the performance is enhanced by drums and flutes:

> We send out the call again
> the drums call the sacred name
> the flutes sing the potent name
> Akataka! Akataka!
> Akataka who wrestled with lion! (p. 12)

The genre of flute and drum produced poetry introduces the praise tradition which provides an insight into the masquerade aesthetic. The masquerade's name („Alakata who wrestled with the lion") is spoken through drum and flute and repeated throughout the poem. The drum and the flute are icons in the traffic into the past to regain that ancient wisdom which the masquerade symbolizes. Hence, we hear the sounds of the sacred drum and flute as the prelude to the voice of the mask:

> The flute calls in the distance:
>
> Call out the masquerade
> Call the fearless spirit;
>
> The drum calls in the distance:
>
> Call the ancient spirit
> Call the past, the present
> Call the future, (p. 14)

As the opening poem of the collection, "A call at dusk" establishes the functions of the masquerade. Here, the masquerade responds to the people's call by restating his commitment to truth: "the lies floating/the masquerade seeking truth" (p. 15).

In "Raising a chant", Ohaeto situates the assertive tone of the masquerade chant within the socio-cultural milieu. Of course this assertiveness derives from the acknowledged role of the masquerade as a spiritual link and symbol of the people's heritage. From this post, the mask speaks with a supreme voice marked in the chant by an authoritative "I". Several poems in Egudu's collection show this assertive voice. A specific example is the Okunaagbaachala masquerade poetry corpus, which Egudu translates literally as "Fire that consumes bamboo" (p. 14). In one of the entries under this corpus, we hear the masquerade's assertive voice making images of his invincibility:

> I, the outcast okra seed
> that outgrew the cultivated one;
> I, a thing grown out of the soil

> which is greater than the one contrived;
> I, the maligned *afo* market
> that is still attended for commerce:
> masquerade that is dreadful!
> I am the thorny herb
> that is never included in soup; (p. 45)

The image is that of a sacred being, whose awesomeness is tempered by the dynamism of his function in social life. As already argued, the masquerade's whole being is rooted in the arena of mediation across all forms of borders – the living and the dead, the ruler and the ruled, the search for harmony and the prevalence of chaos. So, the mask is the manifestation of the invincible force and the will to mediate in conflicting borders. In the Okunaagbaachala corpus, the phenomena of invincibility and will are suggested in the images of the tiger and the snake, "the outcast okra seed" and "the thorny herb". In Ohaeto's poetry, this will derives from the mythic conditioning which for instance makes the masquerade the source of metaphysical powers: "only fortified masquerades/ Brave the nightmare of night" (p. 58).

The rhythm and voice of the masquerade chant are sustained in Ohaeto's collection. In "Raising a chant" for instance, Ohaeto adopts the voice of the masquerade and a repetition technique, which is similar to the kind of parallelism used by Okigbo and Anyidoho. Here, the poet-masquerader announces his arrival:

> I am the tree
> I cannot be climbed,
> I am the earth
> I cannot be carried, (p. 16)

Like the masquerade in the traditional chanting context, the voice in Ohaeto's poem is that of an omniscient, all powerful and all seeing figure speaking as the custodian of the ancestral heritage of the community:

> I am night and darkness,
> I am the one
> they gathered to discuss,
> I am the fly
> I never perch on one sport
>
> I am the third eye
> the invisible one
> If you cannot see me
> Does it mean I cannot see you?
>
> I am the masquerade

> the one they know
> Yet the one they dread...
>
> I say what must be said
> I am the night masquerade
> the one greater than its neighbours, (pp. 16-17)

In tradition, the re-enactment of the mask is also associated with purification rites and the purpose is to cleanse the land of evil so as to sustain hope and harmony in the community. In this regard, Egudu gives the example of the *odo* masquerade, which has

> The salutary secular functions of settling quarrels among people, providing them with recreational activities as well as entertaining displays, and treating them to the pleasurable artistry and the philosophical, social, political as well as moral content of our poetry...like the other types of masquerade, the Nmonwu, his concern in his chants is entirely the well-being of people and the harmony of their society.[42]

In a situation of crisis and despair, the masquerade's will for mediation is required. The transfer of the masquerade's voice into the space of the art of the contemporary artist implies the adoption of the mediation function of which the masquerade poet performs within the society. In "On the street at night", Ohaeto reflects a society in a state of chaos and moral decay. The poet speaks in the "I" mode of the narrator who gives account of personal encounters with people in despair: "I have seen the eyes on the streets/Glow with the drug of despair" (p. 27). The poet sees "a wasted generation" (p. 27) that is consumed by lust and violence:

> they went through universities
> angling for dregs of average joys,
>
> dripping soggy with sampled sex
> insatiable with videos of violence
> they live vicarious foreign lives
> burning hopes in application forms
> listening to the staccato of discos;
> Waste dumps consume their hopes,
> they helled their minds each night
> hallucinating of painted paradise, (p. 27)

In the poem, the voices we hear are those of wanderers, the fragmented individuals whose nights are jostled by nightmares. Using visual and aural

---

[42] ibid: 175.

images, the poet conveys the horror in the voices and actions of girls who sacrifice their youth in sex streets to catch a dream:

> At sunset the girls tumble out
> dreams on shifting sands
> waiting to snatch before sunrise
> Copulating with dollars and sterling
> Catching sunrise on high-rise apartments
> Sometimes dragged away howling
> Waving undressed wind-washed genitals...
>
> Their eyes with fire in their depths
> seek life in wombs of terror
> The despair of unfulfilment closes in
> timing their dripping tears, (p. 28)

In "Night of funerals", the poet uses the metaphor of night to emphasize the deterioration of life in a land where "starved hopes scan the horizon" (p. 28). Here too, hopelessness ("slaughtered hopes", p. 30) exacerbates the contemplation of death and then "lives move in funeral paces" (p. 29). Night and funeral are used repeatedly in the collection. These are symbols which define the atmosphere in a society in a state of misery and fear. Night shelters the prostitutes described euphemistically as "the hawkers of the night" (p. 31) and "the flowers of the night" (p. 31). In the third part of "Night of funerals", we hear the owl's cry piecing through the night "with the dagger of its omen" (p. 32) and "the tremors of panthers" (p. 32) which are "the drums of death" (p. 32).

Ohaeto becomes politically overt as he traces Africa's losses to the problems of leadership:

> The second Sankara slumped
> the minute Murtala died
>> It becomes a night of funerals,
> the hour Nkrumah crumbled
> the day Machel was mangled
>> It became a night of funerals. (p. 33)

In "Each night one fled", the poet paints the picture of an arid country from which everyone is exiled. One notices the poet's attempt to reflect on the exile phenomenon, which characterizes the political struggles of the 90s in Nigeria. There is however a kind of restraint in this portrait for the poet conceals the political subject in the symbol of the desert, a land drained of life. The poem is an allegory on the tense political atmosphere at the height of military despotism in Nigeria when, for most activists and writers, exile was taken as an alternative to execution. At asylum sites, "the rank of rebels swelled" (p. 34) and exiles "gathered/chant across the surging sea" (p. 34) and "A volume of sound reach the desert" (p. 34).

As indicated earlier, the masquerade's traffic through the night is the purification rite that we interpret as act of mediation. The night is the symbol of the horror, which the masquerade must mitigate. In this, the poet constantly reminds us of the sacredness of the masquerade's task and the enormity of the problems to be confronted. In "The chant goes on" for instance, night becomes the symbol of terror:

>It is the terror, the fear
>the pain, the suffering
>the sorrow and the hope
>that fortifies masquerades.
>
>The night waits darkly
>brooding in its silence
>But noisy in its calm;
>In the depth of the night,
>the sullen moon is barricaded
>And the masquerade
>counts the spaces of the missing stars; (p. 58)

The masquerade chant embodies the aesthetic of questioning, searching and censuring. These components of mediation are spelt out in part II of "The chants goes on". The masquerade poet approaches his task through questioning:

>Why are the voices murmuring dirges
>In the womb of this night?
>Chei!
>that is why the masquerade
>>goes at night
>>comes at night
>counting the assembled thoughts...
>
>But must dirges fill the night
>Where the land is so green
>Where the soil drips wealth
>And vegetable ever in bloom?
>Why must dirges fill this night
>>that is why the masquerade
>>must go at night
>>must come at night. (p. 60)

Questioning gives the act of mediation its structure and with this, problems are defined in terms of their origin or nature:

> When the water turns muddy
> we travel to the source
>
> When the smoke ascends
> our eyes turn to the hearth,
>
> When a tree withers
> we search the roots,
>
> That is why the masquerade
> Goes at night
> Comes at night, (p. 59)

The masquerade poet confronts social ills by censuring those who upset the social order. The implication is that those who "hate words of rebuke" (p. 61) are forced to avoid evil. As the voice makes clear, the mask is the icon of social regulation and those who threaten the social fabric are exposed. The poet in the mask of the masquerade does not hesitate to "name the nameless" (p. 61). One of the most articulate expressions of this social control is the description of the function of the mask in the image of the stone which "hangs in the air" to put "the clay pot" (p. 61) in constant fear.

Ohaeto presents the masquerade's link with the earth as a symbolic expression of a commitment to the living. The masquerade unites the dual forms of earthly and spiritual essences. This unity manifests in the paradox: "A birth is death awaited/a death is birth anticipated" ("The living and the dead" p. 14). This interconnection also shows in the lines: "a masquerade must cry/For masquerades also weep" ("The mouth of the night" p. 26). The masquerade's social commitment is reflective of the role of the artist. In "The spirit ties me to this earth", Ohaeto employs the masquerade-earth bond as the symbol for aesthetic mediation. The masquerade that is tied to the earth, who "must walk the land" (p. 36) is engaged in creating the condition for hope:

> But I lay the stones
> I mould the bricks
> I cement the cracks
> For the spirit ties me to this earth.
>
> The voice must rise
> Rise beyond the doubts of this season
> My voice takes fate by the throat
> Shaking it to give a living to the land
> For much an unbroken heart bears
> Much the flesh suffers yet not die. (p. 36)

The Public Voice: The Word as a Scourge

As the discussion shows, the artist's unity with the mask is exemplified in his reconstruction of the chant medium to assume a public voice. This is the major project in *The Voice of the Night Masquerade* where Ohaeto locates the public voice of the Black artist as a continuity from indigenous aesthetic practices. This voice is described in "Planting seeds in the womb of time":

> When you appropriate public wealth
> You owe the public a large debt...
> the bell needs its tongue...
> the voice of the masquerade,
> I talk of going and coming
> I talk of this and that...
> One person is not a public
> But a night masquerade is a public voice (pp. 83-84) act

It is necessary however to restate the fact that the new social context under which the modern poet operates imposes limitation on artistic freedom. This of course affects the artist's will to sustain the critical voice. While comparing the modern poet and the oral artist in this regard, Obiora Udechukwu notes that

> Things have changed. In the traditional society, the artist had protection and there were checks and balances. For instance, you would not dare unmask a masquerade. Unmasking a masquerade was regarded as a terrible offence. In the traditional society, anybody who did that had his house demolished. So, the immunity could hold. But we have moved to a situation where we are no longer operating a purely traditional structure. We are also not operating a purely Western culture where you have a measure of freedom of speech and so on. So, that immunity is not conferred on the artist today and as you have pointed out also, the artist has a signature attached to his work. If Soyinka writes a play what we say is a play written by Soyinka. The government can pounce on him whereas, in the traditional society, the masquerade was a spirit.[43]

Thus, while the critical voice of the oral poet is acknowledged and adopted by the modern poet, the new social structure in which they write inhibits the transfer of the artistic freedom which reflects in the immunity enjoyed by the oral poet.

From what Egudu and Ohaeto reveal to us, the central force in the voice of the masquerade poet is 'the word.' In the masquerade poem, which Egudu translates as "Chanting", we hear the oral poet in the moment of self-praise: "I, the one/in whose mouth words wove their nest!"[44] The masquerade poet takes

---

[43] Charles Bodunde, "Interview with Obiora Udechukwu", *Tape Recording* 18th January 1999, Bayreuth, Germany.

[44] Romanus N. Egudu, *African Poetry of the Living Dead: Igbo Masquerade Poetry: 53.*

pride in his ability to manoeuvre the verbal medium for aesthetic and utilitarian purposes. The creative principle here is one which holds aesthetic quality and innovation as necessary resources in articulating social reality. Again, the masquerade poem "Chanting" exemplifies the oral poet's reference for the word and the ways in which it is manipulated to create the desired impact:

> My words are
> such that are never mastered wholly:
> if you hear what I am saying today
> and you remember what I said long ago,
> you think you have mastered my words.
> But you do not know
> what I will say tomorrow,
> for I am the one
> in whose mouth words have fruited.
> Everybody knows
> that there are words in my mouth,
> for a charmist used my tongue
> to contrive a charm!
> I am the one
> who uses word of mouth
> to harvest hard palm-nuts
> and harvest soft palm-nuts[45]

While using Ayi Kwei Armah's short stories as typical examples, Ode Ogede argues that "the sense of having a mission to teach and to analyse issues of public concern" is obviously "one of the features that, in general, the modern African writer has borrowed from the oral tradition."[46] What needs to be transferred along with this voice is the principle which the oral artist adopts in shaping his aesthetic production and vision. As the corpuses in Egudu's collection reveal, the masquerade poet is conscious of the need to maintain a certain code of conduct in order to act as a credible critical voice:

> For one to be a masquerade medium
> till the aging of the head
> Requires that he will not
> terminate a woman's pregnancy;
> one who does evil things
> cannot be a masquerade medium
> up to old age.[47]

---

[45]ibid: 51.
[46] Ode Ogede, "Oral Echoes in Armah's Short Stories". *African Literature Today* 18, (1992): 73.
[47] Romanus N.Egudu, *African Poetry of the Living Dead: Igbo Masquerade Poetry: 57.*

In *The Voice of the Night Masquerade,* Ohaeto presents the word as the artist's means of mediation. In this text, the word is a motif and the ultimate input in the poet's creativity. The poet builds words into a form, which represents his own mode of cognizing his environment. In "The dancing bee is about to sting", Ohaeto employs the word as input in his quest for social stability. Here, the poet declares:

> Words do not cause dissension
> In the cave of the mouth,
>
> So when a word jumps out
> The answer also drops out, (p. 74)

Words are selected by the artist to produce an effect:

> If I chose my words
> it is not fear not fright
> I make sure the words
> cut close to bone, (p. 78)

The public square is an arena of performance and it is the space where the oral artist re-establishes the tenets of the tradition. Ohaeto reiterates the significance of this platform in lines such as

> The night masquerade assembles
> the secrets on public squares...
> The night is pregnant with memories
> I count our memories and
> I lay them on public squares (pp. 75-76)

Of course, the public square is the symbol of the people's collective experience. To lay memories on this space is to re-enact those historical and cultural experiences that bind the people together as a community. The square communicates a sense of oneness, which is acknowledged and renewed constantly by the run of cultural and aesthetic events. The aesthetic practice of collective participation and renewal of community psyche orientate the people towards the struggle for a society of their vision. The public square is not only an arena for re-enacting the people's aesthetic and cultural experiences. It is an arena for censuring evil and in this sense, satire is the most dominant mode.

The physical and verbal instruments of social regulation are integrated into the paraphernalia of the masquerade. The masquerade uses the cane and the word as the scourge. Ohaeto uses these icons to perform the same censuring function as in the oral tradition. In "Raising a chant", the masquerade carries a cane to punish the deviant:

> Raise a chant for me

> Raise a chant for me
>   the cane carried on a journey
>   the cane carried on a journey
>   Will it end in the bad bush?
>   the cane carried on a journey
>   Must decorate deaf ears. (p. 17)

The masquerade's punishing words (and the words of poets in general) are physicalized in the image of the stinging bees. The image is explored intensely in "The dancing bee is about to sting" where the poet warns:

> the bee is about to sting
> It dances close to deaf ears,
>
> The dog stung by a bee
> Flees at the approach of the fly,
>
> But the head that disturbs the wasp
> invites several stinging replies.
>
> The dancing bee must sting
> the ear must be made to listen (p. 73)

The poet also insists

> The bee will always sting deaf ears...
> The bee has stung deaf ears...
> The bee helped sting deaf ears, (pp. 78-79)

The word, woven as satire, is deployed as a scourge against a leader who deceives and kills

> The bee must sting now –
>
> He came with a grin
> In a flood of flashbulbs
>   they cheered him,
> He caught a kinsman
> Hung a curse on his neck
> Ventilated his torso with bullets
> His blood took many exits
>   And they cheered him,
>
> He shook several hands
> He dribbled several legs
> He tripped in wanton glee
>   still they cheered him, (p. 76)

The people are equally satirized, for their gullibility perpetuate the reign of the tyrant:

> What he gave at the bend
> He took at the roundabout
> Each citadel he touched
> He marked with horror,
>
> But the cheers led him on
> the cheers did not die on time,
> Let the bee sting the cheering ones
> Let the bee sting the cheered one. (p. 76)

The sting metaphor also occurs in "The chant is the escort" where the poet's vitriol against evil-doers is linked with the stinging wasp: "When the wasp wants to sting/It dips its anus into its hive" (p. 39). The point is that Ohaeto's metaphors of the stinging bees and wasp connect the original as shown in the masquerade poem, which Egudu translates as "Toilsomeness":

> I have warned, saying
> that if a head provokes the wasps,
> they will sting it with fury.

The word transmits the essence of a culture and the process of creating and sustaining a viable cultural base requires the wisdom of the word. Ohaeto makes a terse but effective description of the power of the word: "words are shrines of wisdom" ("A chant at the anthole", p. 91). This line is repeated in different contexts throughout the poem. The image of the shrine places word as a sacred verbal phenomenon, which the people cherish as the divine gift of the ancestors. Quite significantly too, the line emphasizes what has been expressed earlier in the discussion as the great capacity of the oral medium to function as the means of sustaining the culture and the continuity of the race.

The artist has a role in the process of cultivating acceptable political culture and he approaches this by reminding the ruling class of its responsibility to the people. As we find in the masquerade poem, "A Newly Crowned Ruler", this political mediation is the legitimate function of the oral artist who addresses the king on behalf of the people:

> I am saying to the king
> that looks after the entire Owa (people),
> Moon that shrines for Owa (people),
> Chief Ozo-Obu:
> let him behave
> like the moon itself:
> let him not destroy a man's yams

> or a woman's coco-yams;
> let him do the work of a chief so well
> that we may use his behaviour
> to boast
> how beautiful Owa (village) is.

On the king's responsibility to the poor, the masquerade's words are:
> Let him defend the poor
> when they are being oppressed;
> let him give them
> what is due to them,
> for to deny a poor person
> what God has reserved for him
> implies that the chief
> is selling his life at auction[48]

As this poem shows, the king is the prime receiver of the masquerade's ancestral wisdom. There is good sense in this for the king is the symbol of the people's collective vision. Ohaeto adopts this mode of intervention in "Raising a chant" where he seems to suggest that a nation may sometimes avoid disaster if the artist has the freedom to execute his sacred task of acting as the people's voice by mediating upon the ruler whose position imposes the important task of protecting the collective vision of his community:

> A crown is a crown
> If a king rules recklessly
> A torn basket adorns our heads
> Then a curse is raised
> for a crown is a crown
> Even crowns of torn baskets. (p. 18)

This idea is sounded again in "Planting seeds in the womb of time" where the poet describes the corrupt in the image of the weed:

> When you appropriate public wealth
> You owe the public a large debt.
>
> I talk loud
> the weed must be uprooted
> The weed ruined the farm (p. 83)

It must be noted that in spite of these enormous problems, the hope for a renewal of life runs in Ohaeto's book. This vision of renewal manifests in the confident proclamation of life by the masked poet-persona after the cleansing rites are accomplished. At the end of "a sacrifice for birth" (p. 96), the word,

---

[48] ibid: 63.

reflecting truth "cleanses the land" (p. 95) and "A land dies then it is born" (p. 95). Still, new life unfolds in the image of "cleansed lands" (p. 96) which "wear green again" (p. 95).

VIII. THE MINSTREL, THE MOURNER AND THE MASK: OBIORA UDECHUKWU'S POETRY

In Obiora Udechukwu's art, what we find is a creative response to the social and political events that impinge on people's daily life. This response is made in his major poetry collection, *What the Madman Said*. In this book, Udechukwu employs the cultural and aesthetic forms of his Igbo background to create a species of poetry that recalls the errors of the past in order to understand the future. The reconstruction of social vision through art requires an imaginative re-engagement and re-interpretation of those oral forms that, for years have served to stabilize the ways people cognise their world. In this connection, Udechukwu acknowledges the role of the minstrel and the epic poet and he approaches these oral artists, borrowing their techniques (metaphors, innuendoes and rhythm) to give vent to personal and public agonies particularly in those poems dealing with the Nigerian civil war:

> What I've also done with poetry is to try and borrow from oral traditions. I've done a lot of work with minstrel and epic poets and I've tried to utilize some of their techniques – the metaphors, the innuendoes which we find in tradition.[49]

In Donatus Nwoga's introduction to *What the Madman Said*, the description of specific borrowed forms indicates Udechukwu's relation with the Igbo oral traditions and the value derivable from such aesthetic transfer:

> "Whirlwind Elegies" which is in honour of Christopher Okigbo and which is declaredly influenced by Christopher Okigbo is yet one of the most authentic poems one could read as a representative of the Igbo poetic tradition. In the tradition of declamatory praise poetry it is structured into overture, salute, and sacrifice; it adopts the performance stance of oral tradition, pointing at and calling upon the praised one (even in his absence through death); above all in the proverbs, wit and imagery of the language it recaptures the traditions of the perceived culture.[50]

The voices we anticipate in *What the Madman Said* are those of the minstrel and the masquerade or the mask. These voices tell the tale of the agony of the ordinary people and chant the praises and dirges of the casualties of war, those "lost in the whirlwind" (p. 11) of political chaos.

---

[49] Charles Bodunde, "Interview with Obiora Udechukwu" *Tape Recording*. 18th January, 1999, in Bayreuth, Germany.

[50] See, introduction, Obiora Udechukwu, *What the Madman Said*. (Bayreuth: Boomerang Press, 1990). All subsequent page references are made to this edition and appear in the text.

The Poet as Minstrel and Mourner

The poem, "Totem of lament" which is written as a prelude to *What the Madman Said* positions the poet as a minstrel, offering songs and music as alternative to violence. This image provides the framework within which the aesthetic and social responsibilities of the poet can be defined. In the prelude, the poet is the optimist who insists on songs and "the festival of flutes" (p. 11), even if "laughter has faded/And the fractured moon, in the aftermath, should/stagger" (p. 11). Thus, the basic theme and aesthetic forms in the collection are previewed in the prelude as renewal of life and this is conveyed in the voice of the itinerant poet whose art is produced to enliven the communities he traverses:

> Let the song still be sung
> In your heart
> Let the song still be sung
> When lights are out (p. 11)

When political crisis results into social disintegration and death, the poet appropriates the traditional dirge as means of response. In Udechukwu's "Whirlwind Elegies" for instance, the crisis of the time turns the poet-minstrel into a mourner and dirge singer. The reflection on death incorporates those conventional forms that the traditional poet employs to express the subject of death. The most relevant forms are the metaphorical rendering of the ecology, culture and symbolic interpretation of cosmic and organic forces to signify on death. These forms have been discussed in relation to the poetry of Christopher Okigbo, Niyi Osundare and Kofi Anyidoho. In reflecting death by constructing parallel images of death in organic and cosmic forms, Udechukwu is intimately linked with the dirge tradition and these poets.

The mourning of the dead reflects solidly in the cosmic images of a sunless sky ("when the eye of the sky is shut", p. 12) and "the roving moon [that] paled behind a screen of solemn cloud" (p. 14). The metaphor of minstrels walking through "the sleeping paths/of …distant farms/seeking the lost flute/By the withered tree" (p. 12) is a subtle reference to the devastation of the agrarian tradition. Specifically, the transferred epithet of "the sleeping path" means that the pathways to farms are empty. This is obviously Udechukwu's own way of recalling the effects of the Nigerian civil war on the life of the ordinary people. The minstrel too has lost his flute to the chaos of the time. Of course, the flute is the symbol of celebration, the festive season and the musical instrument in a masquerade performance. The war situation affects the people's cultural values. For instance, the mask tradition and its vibrant purification rites, songs, music and dance become a ceremony of silence. What this means is that there is a disconnection between the mask and the people. This is symbolic of the destruction of the spiritual harmony and aesthetics that the people have created from their own experience:

> TONIGHT the roving moon paled
> behind a screen of solemn cloud;
> Tonight the masquerade walks
> The dual pathway of the anthole
>
> But there are no drums for the descent
> There are no flutes for his return
>
> And we, dumb as our drums,
> Dumb as our flutes,
>
> Can only moan, silent,
> For him who died but shall not die. (p. 14)

Thus, the metaphor of the lost flute intensifies the grieving mood and the destruction which war has brought on the people's social life. Also in this section of the book, the poet uses the metaphor of the "famished streams" (p. 12) and "desolate lands" (p. 12) as nature imagery to portray the ways in which war erodes human life. Following the dirge tradition of amplifying grief through images of organic decay, Udechukwu employs the metaphors of "sapless stems" (p. 12) and "withered branch" (p. 13) to portray the grey atmosphere of war and death. Throughout "Whirlwind Elegies", the emphasis is on collective grief:

> And we dirge here on sapless stems:
> Young birds before the pregnant hills...
> HERE WE stand
> Two birds on a withered branch
> Here we stand
> Shivering above the burning sands (pp. 12-13)

The gruesome images and sounds of the dying are also collectively felt while the war situation incapacitates all efforts including the basic cultural norm of funeral rites:

> Balls of death scale the distant groves
> Their sounds flow to us muffled by the hills
> And we must sleep with open eyes
>
> Rams fall daily
> And we cannot sing them a dirge

Women and children still drop with hunger and fear:
This is no time for funerary dances. (p. 13)

The mood and focus of the dirge in Udechukwu's book range from general lament to specific grief and from collective mourning to personal loss. The last parts of "Whirlwind Elegies" are devoted to mourning the death of friends and artists during the Nigerian civil war. This section of *What the Madman Said* sustains the dirge convention of celebrating the dead. Again, this aesthetic convention is a product of oral art where dirges are chanted to praise the dead and comment on "the wickedness of death and the futility of life in general."[51]

Christopher Okigbo is evidently the poet on who most dirges have been written by fellow Black poets.[52] In most of the entries in the Okigbo dirge canon, the celebrative tone derives from the allusion to the poet's creative genius and his roots in oral traditions. Udechukwu is influenced by this creative genius in terms of his art and the political vision he displays particularly in the series of poems titled *Path of Thunder*. In this regard, Udechukwu informs that

> Okigbo was a major influence and inspiration in my work and I started writing serious poetry when I encountered his poetry. When we were in the secondary school, we were brought up on British poets. It was only when I had left secondary school that I experienced *Heavensgate* and other Okigbo publications and was then introduced to modern African poetry. Even though I didn't understand his poetry then, it spoke to me. The music and the images affected me directly. That in a way influenced what I have done. The fact that he died for a cause which he believed was right was also my major concern.[53]

Epigraphs and praise poetry are used as techniques in Udechukwu's dirge on Okigbo. These forms occur as quotations or echoes of Okigbo's familiar images and icons in *Labyrinths*. The epigraphs (one each in parts IV and V of "Whirlwind Elegies") are taken from "Initiation" in *Labyrinths*:

> "Except by rooting
> who could pluck yam tubers
> from their base?"(p. 15)

And:

> "The moonman has gone under the sea
> The singer has gone under the shade" (p. 16)

---

[51] Romanus N. Egudu, *African Poetry of the Living Dead: Igbo Masquerade Poetry.* (Lewiston: The Edwin Mellen Press, Ltd., 1992): 25.

[52] See for instance, Chinua Achebe and Dubem Okafor, (eds.), *Don't Let Him Die.* (Enugu: Fourth Dimension Publishers, 1978).

[53] Charles Bodunde, "Interview with Obiora Udechukwu".

The first quotation alludes to Okigbo's strong roots in the culture of his people and the second is written in the form of a personal epitaph that reflects the death of an artist. Of course, these epigraphs (as used by Udechukwu) are useful preludes to Udechukwu's lament of Okigbo's death. The sacrificial ram is one of the most conspicuous symbols in Okigbo's *Labyrinths* especially in the series of poems that deal with war. In "Elegy for Alto" for instance, Okigbo employs the ram symbol to depict the artist as a sacrificial ram, a poetic statement that became prophetic:

> So let the horn paw the air howling goodbye...
> O mother Earth, unbind me; let this be
>   my last testament; let this be
> The ram's hidden wish to the sword the sword's
>   secret prayer to the scabbard[54]

Udechukwu employs the same symbol to echo Okigbo's vision of the critical artist as a sacrificial figure in a society where truth is repressed. Okigbo puts this bluntly in "Hurrah for Thunder": "If I don't learn to shut my mouth/I'll soon go to hell,/I, Okigbo, town-crier, together with my iron bell" (p. 67). Like the poet who refuses to yield to lies, the sacrificial ram is a fitting symbol in expressing the fate and vision of the restless poet who found a role for himself in the Nigerian civil war. Udechukwu makes a subtle reference to this involvement in elegiac tone:

> Today
> you went to battle riding the land,
> But now, carrying that land.
> Ram of the trailing testicles
> Plucked were the organs from their base. (p. 15)

In the final section of "Whirlwind Elegies", subtitled 'Overture', 'Salute' and 'Sacrifice', Okigbo is apostrophised and the core metaphor here is the silencing of a minstrel. In the eye of the mourner-poet, Okigbo is a literary mentor "whose flute sang to us/new songs each moon/without cease" (p. 16). Here again, the flute is used as the symbol for the minstrel-poet. The metaphor of a silenced flute is a variation on the dumb flute imagery in part III of "Whirlwind Elegies". The flute represents the minstrel or generally, the artist. Therefore, the image of a silent flute aptly expresses the death of the artist. The tone in 'Salute' is celebrative and this reflects in the poet's use of organic and cosmic images. Okigbo is the firefly "that left the bad bush/and grew into a star" (p. 16). He is also the shrub "that pierced the forest and knocked the poplars

---

[54] Christopher Okigbo, *Labyrinths*. (London: Heinemann, 1971): 82.

with his jaw" (p. 17). Udechukwu recalls Okigbo's war role in the image of a lunar flute that turns to a gun. This is a more positive view on the controversy that surrounds Okigbo's involvement in the Nigerian civil war. Udechukwu interprets Okigbo's death at the war front as a sacrifice intended to ensure that "future generations/might not bite sand" (p. 17). Seen from the perspective of the artist's public role, the sacrifice is to sustain the committed voice of the artist whose public responsibility correlates with the vision expressed in his art. In a way, Udechukwu alludes to a pattern of immortalized self in Okigbo's art and action. What this means is that the poet still sings (in a life-in-death situation) especially because the force of his art continues to influence other poets who "listen to his flute" (p. 17) and who imagine that

> Somewhere beyond the hills
> The blood of her sunbird
> Merged for ever with sand
> At the confluence of seven seas
> the sunbird and his lioness
> At the confluence of seven deserts
> a new bird takes shape. (pp. 17-18)

In "Aftermath", the minstrel deals with the memories of war. The signs of devastation are everywhere; even the broken floor is "littered with memories of invasion" (p. 22). The poet is a witness to gruesome images of "bones in the tall grass" (p. 22), when the people's hope turns into "hate and rubble" and "where all is rust and decay" (p. 22). The ram symbol occurs here again in form of a local wit: "The ram's mother has no child" (p. 22). This is an apt description of the fate of the ordinary soldier whose position as a man of war implies self-sacrifice. Using the traditional dirge style of the roll call of the dead, Udechukwu recalls the memory of friends lost in war, sacrificed like the ram:

> On my mat, this night,
> Boyhood faces flood my eyes with silent tears –
> NTCHU
> EKULO
> IRUS
> and
> GOMA… faces eyes shall not see again.
>
> On my back,
> Listening in the silent night,
> Stretching my ears across the seven seas…
> But rat's feet on the ceiling
> Are all ears can hear. (p. 23)

Part II of "Aftermath" bears the sense and tone of the dirge. In this section, Udechukwu employs the fallen tree symbol (typical icon in traditional dirge) to express the fall of a race. This is specifically borne out in the image of homeless birds "scattered in the forest" (p. 25) after "THE MIGHTY tree [the race] has fallen" (p. 25). The horror of war and the fall of a race are captured euphemistically in the transferred epithet of mourners who stand before "beheaded palms" (p. 26). Collective sorrow is reflected in the image of a land that is "humming a dirge/humming home the fallen" (p. 26).

The Voice of the Mask

A number of the poems in *What the Madman Said* are written in the voice of the masquerade. Like we find in Ohaeto's *The Voice of the Night Masquerade*, the poet-persona in Udechukwu's book speaks in the assertive voice of the mask. The mask radiates an aura of invincibility that is bestowed on him by tradition. This invincibility manifests in the chant of the mask:

> Maggots or worms cannot touch me...
> I am frog:
> Jumping cannot kill me.
> I am wind:
> Can I succumb to a snare? (p. 39)

The rhythm of the chant is similar to the masquerade (incantatory) formulae, which Ohaeto also employs in "Raising a Chant" where the masquerade-poet declares:

> I am the tree
> > I cannot be climbed
> I am the earth
> > I cannot be carried.[55]

The anthole icon seems to be the most pointed referent, which connects the poet's voice with the sacred voice of the masquerade. In the third stream of "What the Madman Said", the poet affirms:

> My voice calls from a cell
> The voice speaks through cocoon of spider
> My voice declaims from an anthole (p. 41)

The anthole icon reflects the Igbo mythology in which masquerades are believed to inhabit antholes. Again, this same icon appears in Ohaeto's "A chant at the anthole" to reflect this myth:

---

[55] Ezenwa-Ohaeto, *The Voice of the Night Masquerade*. (Ibadan: Kraft Books, 1996): 16.

> Masquerades emerge from antholes
> Masquerade depart through antholes,
> the night masquerade is at the anthole. (p. 91)

In the mask tradition, truth is held sacred and the rituals and chants of the masquerade are the traditional means of emphasizing it. Udechukwu re-affirms this principle in metaphorical terms:

> TRUTH IS iron
> is my A.D.C.:
> Truth is pregnancy:
> You cannot hide it at nine months (p. 39)

Since the modern artist does not have the kind of immunity that the masquerade enjoys, he adopts the mask (or courage) of the madman to speak about the evils in his society. Madness in this case is metaphoric, for as Ohaeto argues, "the Igbo perceive madness as a state in which an individual could condemn evil without fear of punishment".[56] Udechukwu defends the artist's mask of madness seeing it as a medium through which the actions of despots could be questioned:

> Be NOT amazed
> If they call you mad
> Do not rage
> If they call you fool
> > call you names
>
> For the madman sees
> The spirit lurking in the dark
> The madman perceives
> What only eyes of dogs can film
>
> The madman sees
> The question among the dark clouds
> The question that questions their stool. (p. 40)

The poet finds enough reasons to tell the truth of his society for everywhere,

> The question looms in the evening cloud
> It hangs so it's now part of the sky
> The question their chiefs do not want to see
> The question that questions their stools (p. 60)

---

[56] Ezenwa-Ohaeto, *Contemporary Nigerian Poetry and the Poetics of Orality*. (Bayreuth: Bayreuth African Studies, 1999): 122.

In a period of great suffering, there is an urgent need for mitigation and the artist requires the will of the masquerade to locate the cause of social rupture. Thus, like the masquerade, the contemporary artist performs the role of raising people's consciousness towards social construction. In this context, Udechukwu defines the function of the artist in the symbol of the cock, which warns about the passage of time in a temporal world where posterity judges us according to how timely we intervene to humanize our world. The link between the artist and the lunar cock shows in the lines:

> I am the one speaking!
> If I do not wake the cock,
> The cock will not wake the sun.

This link is used by the poet as an argument against the censorship of the contemporary artist:

> IF WE KILL the cock that crows
> Who will now rouse the sun from sleep?
> If we kill the bird that sings
> Who will distil harmonies from the clouds?
>
> Question I address to our people:
> Question I address to the land:
> Question I address to the world:
>   If they kill a star
>   Can they fashion another star? (p. 64)

Meanwhile, the only signs that the poet sees around him are those of chaos and decay. These signs reflect the horror perpetrated by self-declared messiahs:

> A terrible wind is howling at the gate of the city
> A monster is shaking the dam across the fabled river
> And a nation is wobbling on
> The people are staggering
> Drowning in the sea of fart
> These saviours have anointed
> The uniformed caste that bestrides the land
> From the Niger to the Indian Ocean…
> We are passing
> The saviours are passing
> Owners of the people are passing
> Tax-eaters are passing (pp. 43-44)

Udechukwu explores the ironic situation of a madman who is the lone voice of sanity. Against the pervading insanity only the poet (the madman in the public eye) perceives the general chaos:

> I saw locusts darkening the sky
> I told the mongrels newly drunk on oil
> I told them that I saw death at Afo market
> That I tremble at what I saw with my two eyes
> But they laughed
> Called me a madman (p. 44)

The poet is evidently worried by the general decay of social facilities around him and he is even more disturbed by a public that is incapable of perceiving this decay. His local sarcasm on this problem fails to register in the public mind:

> I went to the city
> Asked them to search for the black goat
> Before sundown
> There is no night in the city, they said
> And they laughed at me (p. 44)

The poet behind the mask sees all the contradictions around him: "Electric light died in the city/And taps went on sympathy strike" (p. 42). Petroleum wealth does not improve the life of the ordinary people; instead, it brings corruption and poverty. The poet presents a different kind of mask in the image of the "immaculate chief" (p. 48) who is simply "an invisible cheat" (p. 48) behind the disguise. Moral corruption is expressed in terms of the loss of beauty:

> I DO NOT pause on my way to work
> For the flowers are gone
> I do not pause on my way to market
> For the flowers are gone (p. 49)

Social decay is also indicated in the images of filth and apathy: "Dustbins overflow like the Niger/And Sanitary will not arrest you" (p. 54).

Throughout the section titled "What the Madman Said", one hears the voice of the masked poet criticizing all forms of corruption. He lashes out at generals, false heroes who "have taken more titles /and retired" who "have taken more wives/and gone to bed" (p. 52). Corrupt politicians are also roundly criticized for their false promises, words that are "spoken to the wind" (p. 52). The poet's mask is a shield, which protects him from the afflictions of the corrupt. The mask is also the all-seeing eye with which he reads the intentions and actions of those who corrupt the land:

> They offered me crumbs
> Thinking I would sing their praises
> If they shut their doors on me
> I say
> If they shut their doors on me

97

> Have they also shut my eyes?
>
> If you shackle my feet
> Have you manacled my ears?
> If you pinion my arms
> Have you manacled my tongue?
>
> Stealing gave them the eagle feather
> Robbery gave them the ankle-string
> Killing gave them the bronze staff
> Tax eating gave them their carved stools (pp. 54-55)

The mask is the sacred memory of the past. Therefore, this is a reliable traditional medium of re-enacting the people's historical experience. The poet weaves the contradiction in this experience into chanted refrains:

> We were once poor but wealthy
> We are now rich but poor...
>
> We were once poor but rich
> We are now rich but poor...
>
> Better to be mad and free
> Than to be rich and blind...
>
> We were once poor but happy
> We are now rich but hungry...
>
> We were once naked but alive
> We are now clothed but a corpse (pp. 53-55)

This binary line formation, which is designed to reveal the antithesis of wealth and poverty; freedom and blindness; life and death, provides the appropriate summary for the art and vision, which emerge in Udechukwu's poetry.

IX. *IVWIE, IVWRI* AND *EDON*: TANURE OJAIDE AND THE URHOBO TRADITION

Tanure Ojaide's vision of reality is constructed out of an oral aesthetic to which he is evidently connected. His relation with orature is informed by the belief that a people's aesthetic embodies those cultural and historical experiences that define their reality. For Ojaide, the oral art derives its relevance and communicativeness through a constant re-enactment of those experiences, which affirm the people's culture and history.[57]

Given the extent of the leadership crisis in Black nations at the moment, Ojaide believes that the artist could make a more meaningful intervention in his society by relocating oral forms like satirical songs into the written text. He speaks specifically of *udje* song mode, which is dominant in his Urhobo aesthetic:

> I grew up in an *udje* environment. These are satirical songs, songs of lamentation and are at times a few praises. When you have this kind of corpus and with what has been happening in Nigeria for the past thirty years, there is a lot one could do with this traditional form especially in criticizing the evils in our present system. You know *udje* is itself a satirical genre. In traditional society, satire is a form of social control. So if you want to make social deviants fall within the norm you have to sing a satire about them. One way of approaching what has been going on in African countries is to use this medium to expose the wrong-doers. So, *udje* is an appropriate artistic medium especially in this period in Africa.[58]

Udje defines Ojaide's critical voice and the need to create an effective satirical mode provokes the poet into re-investing certain Urhobo symbols and cultural practices with meanings and interpretations, which connect contemporary realities. These symbols and practices are *Ivwie, Ogiso, Iwvri* and *Edon*. Ojaide's *The Fate of Vultures and Other Poems* and *Invoking the Warrior Spirit* are central in discussing these socio-aesthetic patterns.

---

[57] Tanure Ojaide, *Poetic Imagination in Black Africa: Essays on African Poetry*. (Durham: Carolina Academic Press, 1996): 17.
[58] Charles Bodunde, "Interview with Tanure Ojaide" *Tape Recording*. 12th March, 1999, Fez, Morocco.

The Cries of *Ivwie*

Aesthetic transfer goes beyond mere physical transfer. The artist requires a knowledge of the social and aesthetic practices of the culture from which he is borrowing and the ways in which these practices have changed over time. In making an aesthetic interpretation of the Urhobo *Ivwie* concept, Ojaide first defines the principle in terms of its social relevance:

> The concept of *Ivwie* is as old as the Urhobo people and their land. When an individual, a family, or a community felt blatantly victimized, oppressed, denied basic rights, and rendered helpless without any provocation, the person or group cried for justice to the larger community or town that was honour-bound to rescue the aggrieved from the humiliation. The individual was, of course, part of the family, and the family part of the community so that the problem was considered not personal but communal. Once the cry, *Ona na ivwie* (This is unprovoked victimization), was raised, the resources of the group were harnessed to seek immediate redress for the aggrieved.[59]

As Ojaide makes clear, the *Ivwie* principle is hinged on community will and its purpose is to preserve social justice. The poet's concern in this is the ways in which current realities become disruptive of the *Ivwie* principle of communal essence. This concern is expressed in *Invoking the Warrior Spirit* from the viewpoint of a poet-persona who makes a sweep through a people's tragic history. In this respect, the poet reflects the extent to which incidents of injustice, victimization, state oppression and human rights abuse have destroyed the people's collective will.

In the *Ivwie* section of *Invoking the Warrior Spirit*, the signs around the poet indicate ethnic tension and suspicion. The *Ivwie* spirit is lost and the community is taken over by "strangers invoking kites and crows" (p. 47). The combination of predatory and carrion images indicates anti-community phenomenon reflecting both the capacity for destructiveness and the decay of values. The poet raises alarm at the danger posed by the new predatory culture. It replaces the broader humanistic values of communal practice with narrow ethnic chauvinism:

> Even when I stay at home,
> strangers invoking kites and crows
> torch my roof – they will go
> so far to offer burnt offerings.
> And going out of my delta ways,
> indigenes swearing by their land

---

[59] Tanure Ojaide, *Invoking the Warrior Spirit*. (Ibadan: Heinemann, 1998): xi-xii. All subsequent page references are made to this edition and appear in the text.

> deny me hospitality – they fear
> that I will make their ground
> my springboard to riches. (p. 47)

The traditional means of sustaining social cohesion breaks down under ethnically induced violence:

> That's how I knew neighbours in bleak days –
> none would take us in, their religion stopped
> at cursing the assailant and calling for revenge.
> How could we be neighbours of the top
> from our tin homes, how could our calico
> fit into caste of brocade?

Ivwie is a mechanism of social control and it is a matter of grave concern for the poet that the new social reality neither makes provision for the continuity of the tradition nor creates alternative means of sustaining social justice. Thus, abuse of power is constantly displayed in terms of the violation of the rights of the ordinary people. Ojaide defines this problem using the analogy of the predatory relation of the self-deified tyrant imaged as the hawk that "seeks out fowls" (p. 48). The poet describes the experience of the victimized in the image of cockroaches crying *Ivwie* against predatory cocks. Here too, it is the poet who speaks on behalf of the victimized, reflecting a void in social justice and asking for an *Ivwie* intervention in a rhetorical tone: "who will save roaches from/poaching cocks of the court? /Who has no right to life?" (p. 48).

The absence of intervention creates an amoral cult in which power and control are determined by the superiority of killing agents:

> Assailants came with stetsons and magnums,
> we threw sticks and assegais at them;
> our weapons fell short of the distance
> the enemy knew how to contract with lead. (p. 49)

As the poet shows, the victimized are trapped inescapably in the fear created by the men of guns who control the state. The victimized are the ordinary people who are displaced or fragmented for ethnic or economic reasons. Their experiences are captured in images reflecting broken psyche. They are portrayed as terrorized and "muffled by loud reports/ that spill blood over the palaver of minds" (p. 49). In the absence of justice, the land "has been bent like an iron rod" (p. 49) to crush the defenseless who are already "disabled by fortune" (p. 49). In establishing the fate of the victimized, Ojaide employs the iroko tree icon which in oral aesthetic signifies conquest and domination. The poet's technique of image-making is derived from oral poetry where the iroko symbol occurs in association with the contra-image of the diminutive shrubs:

> I, who shelter from the canopy of the iroko tree

> that deflects the eye from the mass of shrubs,
> suffer the absence of recognition, the erased mark
> of roots that could not taunt the sky
> with pointed fingers. I am a minority
> in the massive tower of light-blessed leaves. (p. 53)

This technique is linked with what has been noted in Niyi Osundare's "Akintunde come Home", where the mythical aura of the iroko tree is deployed to reveal the mystification and conquest of the weak by the powerful.

As the poet explains, the prevailing culture of graft is a product of the "short-sighted Vision" (p. 58) of power seekers who "are gone mad and have become/cavalries that crush the land" (p. 58). Ojaide berates leaders and followers in the cult of the corrupt describing them as desecrators of the sacred core of communal well-being:

> Front-runners set patterns of foolhardy greed,
> they took from the sacred chest communal cash.
> Blind to forbidden ways, they ran into evil alleys
> deaf to shouts of restraint and self-sacrifice;
> they fed themselves fat in the neck and thigh
> and set themselves as a caste of renegade priests,
> despoilers of their proclaimed mascot. (pp. 58-59)

Part VI of the section on *Ivwie* is devoted to the idea of recreating the environment and the question of social justice. Natural agencies and animal imagery are employed to reflect the ideas of reconstruction and justice. For instance, we hear "the wind that blows away the falcon's eggs" (p. 55), the ocean current "that returns the tortoise for trial" (p. 55), the crab which creates a hole that "will be haven from drought" (p. 55) and "the donkey that throws down its doomed rider" (p. 55). In the present circumstance, these kinds of intervention are lacking in the poet's own world. Thus, these symbolic actions are used in contemplating the magnitude of the decay of justice and creative impulse in contemporary life.

With a decadent culture that makes *Ivwie* unworkable, the poet seeks a substitute in his own voice believing that a poet's word, like the voice of the singer "scares off stalkers" (p. 55). The evil of injustice needs to be destroyed in order to restore the crushed psyche of the victimized and prepare the ground for social construction. As the poet puts it, "Injustice/deserves to be flared to ashes/to heal the wound of victims" (p. 52). Anger turns into curses as the poet invokes lightning to "cut down those/who netted the destinies of others/into their pot bellies!" (p. 52).

The experience in the *Ivwie* section of *Invoking the Warrior Spirit* could easily be read as a lament. The real focus however, is on the re-awakening of the *Ivwie* principle to humanize the environment. This is consistent with what the poet envisions in the preface to *Invoking the Warrior Spirit* as mediating the present disruption by deploying certain elements of traditional institutions and practices:

> Contemporary Africans have ignored the legacy of traditional institutions, philosophy and art, which can help them confront individual and communal problems. We give too much time to elegies and dirges as if Africa is dying or already dead. We need commemoration of our legacies not only in art works but as an invocation for those qualities we need now more than at any time past for our well-being and survival. The surviving virtues bequeathed on us will ensure our own survival. (pp. xii-xiii)

Ogiso and the *Ivwri* Mythology

The poet retains the image of the past by weaving the actions of characters in myth, history or folklore into the space of poetry. Often, the poet reconstructs the image of his subject in an epic genre, which as we find in Kunene's example of a re-interpretation of Shaka, the epic subject becomes a hero who employs all strategies to prosecute his vision of a nation. Sometimes, the intention of the hero is less controversial as we find in the glowing celebration of the mythical hero in Osofisan's transposition of Orunmila (*Ifa*) mythology in *Dream Seekers on Divining Chain*. With Ojaide's *Ogiso*, history is revisited to present the image of an anti-hero. This is probably more realistic given the fact that the available political events around the poet do not reflect that there are heroes to celebrate. Furthermore, Ojaide's image of the anti-hero ought to be situated in the context of the *udje* (satirical) genre, which influences much of the poems in the collections being discussed. In a footnote to *Edon* in section three of *Invoking the Warrior Spirit*, Ojaide explains that among the Urhobo people, *Ogiso* refers to the „infamous Benin tyrant who made them [the Urhobo] flee to their present Delta area" (p. 31). An earlier description of this figure appears in a footnote to "Elegy for nine warriors" (*Delta Blues & Home Songs*), Ojaide's poem on the execution of Ken Saro Wiwa and eight other Ogoni leaders. In the poem, Ojaide explains that *Ogiso* is the "legendary tyrant in Urhobo and Edo folklore" (p. 29). *Ogiso* survives in Ojaide's poetry as the icon of tyranny. This phenomenon is constructed in poetry as an archetypal pattern which embodies mythic or folklore characters and contemporary despots identified as corrupt politicians or military men who gun their way into power. In the poem titled

"The funeral of the hyena" (*The Fate of Vultures & Other Poems*), Ojaide uses the devouring rage of the hyena as a metaphor for Ogiso archetypal plunder:

> if you catch *Ogiso*
> on the raw side of the throne
> stealing into you with malice
> thirsty for blood-draughts
> patient for your death
> and you cry out
> that he's not composed
> for the likes of
> scorpions
> hyenas
> vultures
> they aren't the street salt
> nor their rule a refuge[60]

As argued earlier, *udje* is the appropriate aesthetic means of reflecting the *Ogiso* image. In *The Fate of Vultures and Other Poems*, the strident voice of the satirist appears in three or four instances in which the *Ogiso* symbol is located. In "The funeral of the hyena" for instance, the poet lashes against *Ogiso* who disguises himself in the mask of a hero. In "Stone culture", *Ogiso* the tyrant is demonized. He is associated with primitive tactics, "the stone culture of power" (p. 30). He rages across "stiff hillocks" and "mangoes planted on their chest" leaving the land "eternally ruined" (p. 30). To assume the *udje* form is to take up the social function associated with it. Ojaide's charge to the artist is that he must find the courage to tell the *Ogisos* of this world how filthy they are:

> leap like a deer
> in the shadow of arrow-heads
> into a cloud
> blaze a rut of clout
> for there's no other shield
> with hit-seeking points
> roaming the savannah for you
> for telling *Ogiso*
> what you see through;
> a mountain of filth. (p. 73)

Ojaide's title poem, "The Fate of Vultures" is evidently one of the most coherent satires against the corrupt ruling class. The poem is reviewed elsewhere as an intense exposé of corruption among politicians in Nigeria's second attempt

---

[60] Tanure Ojaide, *The Fate of Vultures & Other Poems*. (Lagos: Malthouse Press Ltd., 1990)

at democratic rule.[61] Ojaide invokes *Aridon*, god of memory on corrupt politicians, the *Ogisos* who "consume and scatter" and "shared contracts in cabal" (p. 11). In "Elegy for nine Warriors" (*Delta Blues & Home Songs*) Ojaide describes the military *Ogiso* as a savage in a thoroughly devastating lampoon:

>The butcher of Abuja
>dances with skulls,
>Ogiso's grandchild by incest
>digs his macabre steps
>in the womb of Aso Rock.[62]

The *Ivwri* mythology is built around the Urhobo fighting spirit and what Ojaide does is to weave this form into a poetry of invocation and a battle call against *Ogisos*, those he describes as "a plagued dynasty of beasts" who should not "be allowed to live a full life" (p. 17). The myth of *Iv*wri is fully described in the preface to *Invoking the Warrior Spirit*:

>*Ivwri*, a battle-god, was created and invoked by the Urhobo people of Nigeria's Delta during the slave-raiding period. *Ivwri* was then invested in a carving, part human, part animal with many icons that defined the fighting spirit of the people ... Harassed by incessant raids by Europeans and their middlemen, the Urhobo people fought with their machetes against foreign guns... This feat is remembered in the art work which has survived from that period to this day. No period after the slave-raiding centuries has needed *Ivwri* more than now to eliminate the many obstacles in Africa's way. (p. x)

The *Ivwri* section, which informs the title of the collection opens with the poet's image of the loss of vision. Here, the healer, the eagle and the hunter are used as symbols in presenting the poet's concern for the people's failing courage and vision:

>If the healer's favorite child dies,
>know that he has expended his resources.
>
>If the eagle fails to soar to the sky,
>what features will perch on the iroko tree?
>
>If the hunter runs away from night,
>who will bring us the prize game? (p. 5)

Ojaide turns from the general to the specific and locates the focus of his poetry within his Delta background. The Delta riverine and forest settings appear in the images of river beaches where the "mirrored cans and icons/of cult

---

[61] Charles Bodunde, "Review of The Fate of Vultures: New Poetry from Africa". *Research in African Literatures* 22, 3 (Fall 1991): 185.
[62] Tanure Ojaide, *Delta Blues & Home Songs*. (Ibadan: Kraft Books Ltd., 1997): 26.

devotees" (p. 9) are flung. The friendly boat driver "made the Delta/ a family of creeks, fish provider/that filled every mouth" (p. 9). The poet paints a landscape of enthralling beauty, the Delta of

>Evergreen magnate
>whose close weave
>catches the sun
>and leaves leftovers
>of light to slip
>through its sieve! (p. 11)

The poet's Delta is far from a romanticized landscape. It is a landscape of antithesis where "thorns/have brought tetanus" and life made difficult by "colonies of bees" (p. 11) and wasps. From the palm tree of this landscape, "the tapster fell, dead" (p. 11) and "puffaders and scorpions/ refuged under "the leaf/mat of [its] tangled locks/have brought fame/and wealth to healers" (p11). Here too, "Shell BP flared/the forest into a wasteland" (p. 12) in its exploitative rage. Thus, the poet becomes a witness to a ruined landscape where the *Ivwie* cry for justice against *Ogisos* is lost.

The situation dictates that there is a greater need for the individual to undergo self-searching and a re-awakening from what the poet perceives as collective atrophy. The poet first seeks a symbolic union with *Ivwri*, the fighting god, in order to recollect his sanity and rebuild his fragmented self. He does this through the medium of invocation:

>I have ridden the iguana
>and mounted the hornbill,
>brought together two spirits
>into one necessary god.
>I have called *Ivwri* to the shrine...

>Buffalo that drives bush farers
>from its dominion of leaves,
>Crocodile that polices the water
>from the river to the sea,
>Eagle, marshal of the sky,
>that supervises our airspace,
>from your conglomerate of power,
>Great *Ivwri*, you who cannot
>be fully known, give me
>enough to be firm and free. (p. 16)

The poet's appeal to mythology does not necessarily amount to seeking metaphysical resolution of problems, which are pointedly social. Myth is employed here as a means of connecting the past with the present and the *Ivwri* myth, which is itself an icon of the collective essence functions in Ojaide's poetry as the index of renewed collective psyche. This appears in the enthusiastic voice of the poet:

> *Ivwri* waits at the bottom of the precipice
> to cushion us against a hard fall
> *Ivwri* fortifies the threatened with *utiri*
> that blunts the blades of machetes,
> *Ivwri* keeps the gun from firing at his devotees,
> *Ivwri* snatches his favorites from peril
> and throws them into safety. (p. 17)

Re-inventing the *Edon* Vision

As we have seen, the major concern in Ojaide's poetry relate to the question of the failure of social and political institutions. In this, the past is used as a referent signifying the poet's attempt to mediate the present by reconnecting it with certain valuable practices of the old tradition. To this extent, Ojaide makes an imaginative recast of Urhobo traditional political practice particularly in *Invoking the Warrior Spirit* where the palace ceremony of initiation into the throne is transposed. The *Edon* institution is the poet's means of cultivating the past. This tradition is described in the context of its relevance to contemporary political realities:

> Rulership in Africa has led to excesses of tyranny and corruption, which are currently Africa's ravaging plagues. Measures were instituted long ago to curb these excesses. The traditional institution of Edon in Ughelli, perhaps derived from *Uselu* of ancient Benin, trains the would-be *Ovie* on the do's and don'ts of rulership. The student prince has to spend three lunar months confined to a secluded house by which former rulers were buried... Elders, priests, priestesses, and chiefs give him lessons about taboos and service. There he learns the different sacrifices he must make to be in good standing with his gods and people. Before he gets installed as king, he watches the women perform the broom dance, the symbolic importance of which sinks into his head... Hence the protagonist of the poem here, an aspirant to rulership, goes to *Edon* to train to be a worthy ruler. (p. x-xi)

The would-be king is a potential mediator. His task of mending the environment involves a special kind of journey embarked upon in a state of retreat. We find this variant of the journey archetype in Kunene's image of Shaka's journeys (which are physical and mental). Perhaps the more revealing type occurs in Soyinka's portrait of Ogun's pilgrimage into rock shields. Like in these cases, *Edon* retreat reflects the archetypal pattern of the potential mediator in a journey into self-discovery. The journey into the unconscious in the state of the *Edon* retreat is the moment in which the pilgrim-prince discovers his own nature and defines the complex task of mediation. In this connection, Ojaide presents the voice of the pilgrim-prince who defines *Edon* as

> ... learning across
> the board, going beyond borders
> to secure the communal land
> put under my care. (p. 29-30)

In the *Edon* retreat, the principles of mediation are structured as patterns of symbols. The poet expresses Edon principle of equality in animal symbols:

> I have been taken to a colony
> where I couldn't tell king
> among ants in their hauling business.
> I have been to the city of catfish
> and seen equality not just in beards,
> and yet they have *Okobaro* (p. 30)

Certain qualities must reflect in the personality of a leader. For this reason, the *Edon* pilgrimage is organized as an institution where sensitive minds and selfless service are cultivated. As the poet-protagonist apprehends the symbols and the knowledge which unfolds before him, he is able to appreciate the fact that "the high stool of governance/must bear the land's offering/through mountains" (p. 21) and the genuine throne seeker must "prepare the soul/to hear cries locked in stone,/and foresee the light/lodged in dark clouds" (p. 22). The *Edon* learning environment challenges the intending ruler into a unity with his people and landscape:

> I must know from skulls
> names of my forebears,
> I must commit to memory
> the entire line of bloodkins.
>
> From this observatory,
> I know my chiefdom;
> from the green coastline
> to the brown Sahel,
> I map out the landscape
> of my dreary task. (p. 24)

Certain ritual acts within the *Edon* institution are enacted to communicate the ways in which despots are treated. Ojaide presents these ritual acts as symbolic means of regulating power. For instance, the broom dance for the pilgrim-prince is symbolic of the people's rejection of a king who becomes too power conscious; with "a flame in the head" (p. 25). Such a king is deposed through the people's collective action. He is swept out "like dirt out of their sight" (p. 27). The poet extends the power motif by drawing upon folk wisdom communicated through animal imagery:

> If you elect rats to guard your property,
> know you have blessed a clan of thieves;
> if the ram is ordained priest,
> let the maids beware... (p. 26)

The *Edon* platform is for creating the correct attitude to governance and for this reason, it stands to negate the *Ogiso* cult. Ojaide articulates this in rhetorical term:

> Who wants to go down *Ogiso's* line
> and preside over a citizenry of cadavers?
> Who wants to be a hyena in the national palace
> and laugh at the bite in the market? (pp. 23-24)

As the poet-persona expresses it, what *Edon* envisions is a political state in which leaders actively come to terms with the demands of their position; having the will to "look out beyond bends and stretches/into taking those behind home" (p. 30) and the courage to put the verbal declaration into practice: "count me out of the mis-/appropriating game that leaves/my people out in the cold" (p. 31).

As argued earlier, Ojaide's vision operates at social and political frontiers and oral aesthetic forms; traditional institutions are engaged in projecting the ideals he envisions along these frontiers. As the discussion indicates, the sections on *Ivwri* and *Ivwie* reflect the *udje* as an aesthetic means of exposing negative behaviour. The section on *Edon* focuses on the traditional form of humanizing the institution of rulership. Looking at both *Ivwri* and Edon from this perspective, one finds two levels of mediation. One is the mythologized expression of psychic recovery at individual and collective fronts. This of course involves a symbolic (or imaginative) interpretation of the *Ivwri* mythology. The other level is an invented political (or cultural) institution in which potential political mediators (in this particular case, the prince, heir to the throne) are themselves mediated upon through a structured programme of learning. These explorations in mythology and socio-political institutions define the oral roots of Ojaide's poetry and establish his voice as a convincing interpretation of contemporary experiences.

X. ORAL AESTHETICS AND THE BLACK CARIBBEAN POET: KAMAU BRATHWAITE AND THE AFRICAN IMAGE

The Black presence in the Caribbean manifests in the survival of certain aesthetic and cultural practices associated with the Black African world. David Nichol, among others, provides interesting examples of remnants of African aesthetics and culture in diaspora settings:

> In Haiti, African gods were transferred into Roman Catholic saints in Voodoo ceremonies, in Surinam, traces of the Temne of Sierra Leone and the Ashanti of Ghana remain; in a remote village of Trinidad, an old lady reminisced about her grandmother in the 19th century who danced in the rain during thunderstorms and sang praises to Shango, the Nigerian Yoruba god of lightning and thunder.[63]

The spirit of racial solidarity and assertion flourishes well among a group, which possesses a cohesive set of cultural values. However, years of separation from Africa and alienation from the new world of the Caribbean created an exile condition for the Black diaspora. The explosive social and political activities in the middle of the twentieth century gave rise to new waves of cultural consciousness, especially in multicultural societies like the Caribbean and the United States of America. What Michael Furay says about the condition that impelled Pan-African sensibility in the African-American relates to the African-Caribbean condition. Furay observes that

> The new Negro's estrangement from American society made their symbolic journey to Africa inevitable, for they lived and worked in the United States unlike the many white writers of the avant-garde who opted to become exiles in the capital city of Europe. When their repudiation of white America failed to close measurably the gap between the promise and the practice of democracy, their longing for distant Africa ... became more pronounced.[64]

Alienation and deculturalization impelled a critical and practical search for identity among the African-Caribbeans. The most significant representation of this search was the *Négritude* movement pioneered by the Caribbean poet Aimé Césaire and his West African counterpart Léopold Sédar Senghor. Césaire explains the spirit behind *Négritude* in an interview with Charles Rowell:

> *Négritude* was for us a way of asserting ourselves. First, the affirmation of ourselves, of the return to our identity, of the discovery of our own selves. It was

---

[63] Nichol, Davidson, "The African and the Jewish Diasporas: A Comparative Study". *Présence Africaine* 114 (1980): 179.

[64] Michael Furay, "Africa in Negro American Poetry to 1929". *African Literature Today* 1-4 (1972): 32.

in no way a racist theory. *Négritude* provided me with clues in order to read Martinique, its mirror.[65]

He identifies the rallying force of *Négritude* as "this desperate quest for ourselves, this feeling of a faithfulness towards our 'ancestors'."[66] Césaire also admits that the American Black Renaissance was a positive influence on the philosophical and aesthetic movement of *Négritude* because it set in motion "the beginning of a cultural revolution, a kind of revolution of values".[67] The idea of cultural revivalism and rehabilitation, envisioned in the socio-cultural format of *Négritude* continued in the US-influenced Caribbean Black Power movement of the seventies. The vision of the Black solidarity movement in the Caribbean is captured in the following excerpt from a speech made by a Black leader:

> This vision has prompted an entry into the cultural history of black profile in the effort to rediscover our essences, our real selves. That search has resulted in the important realisation that these principles, which inform traditional black societies need to be reaffirmed because of their essential humanistic character. Such reaffirmation we consider vital to the resolution of the spiritual crisis that bedevils black subjugated peoples.[68]

Cultural awareness and racial pride are propagated in order to create the necessary condition for cultural reconstruction, an aesthetic project that E.N. Obiechina describes as "cultural nativism."[69] The significance of imaginative transfer of cultural products in Black literature is underlined by Houston A. Baker Jr. in his evaluation of criticism relating to Black aesthetics:

> The corpus of Black American literature might be defined as that body of written works crafted by authors consciously (even, at times, self-consciously) aware of the longstanding values and significant experiences of their culture. By embodying these experiences and values in expressive form, the writer provides one means through which those who share the same culture can recognize themselves and move toward fruitful self-definition. The literature contains deep aspects of the culture, and its black audience actively benefits from its reflection of the most humane values of a singular whole way of life.[70]

---

[65] Charles H. Rowell, "Interview with Aimé Césaire". *Callaloo: Journal of Afro-American and African Arts* 12, 38 (1989): 55.

[66] ibid: 63.

[67] ibid: 51.

[68] Cited in Ramesh Deosaran, "Some Issues in Multiculturalism: The Case of Trinidad and Tobago in the Post-Colonial Era". *Caribbean Quarterly* 33, 1 (March-June 1982): 62.

[69] E. N. Obiechina, "Cultural Nationalism in Modern African Creative Literature". *African Literature Today* 1-4 (1972): 25.

[70] Houston A. Baker, Jr., "On the Criticism of Black American Literature: One View of the Black Aesthetic". *Cornell University African Studies and Research Center Monograph Series* 4 (1976): 48.

Kamau Brathwaite assumes the typical role of representing the Black world in a literary medium. The assumption here is that this poet, like many of his contemporaries in the Caribbean literati, is motivated to envision the Black world as a result of his enthusiasm for cultural recovery and re-affirmation in the atmosphere of competitiveness and racial suspicion induced by multicultural formation. The concern in this chapter is to investigate Brathwaite's trilogy, *The Arrivants*, in order to determine how he sustains his image of the Black world in terms of culture, history and aesthetics.

Cultural Dislocation and the Search for Racial Origin

The three parts of *The Arrivants* – *Rights of Passage, Islands* and *Masks* – are designed to comment on the African-Caribbean experience. The series of poems in *Rights of Passage*, for instance, emphasize the circumstances that created the existing problem of cultural dislocation. The speaker in "New World Acoming" expresses the collective agony of a violated race. There is a nostalgic recollection of the African past leading to reminiscences of the organized physical violence that accompanied the enslavement of the Black race and the consequent attrition of its culture in the New World. The speaker presents the scene of slaves traversing a rugged landscape, in order to convey the physical and mental agony that mark the violent history of Africa:

> How long have we
> travelled down
> valleys down
> slopes, silica
> glinted, stone
> dry as water,
> to this flash
> of flame in the forest.[71]

The disorientation and hopelessness experienced in the New World are mediated in an emotive tone that reveals collective psychic dislocation:

> O who now will help
> us, help-
> less, leader-
> less, no
> Hawkins, no

---

[71] Edward Kamau Brathwaite, *The Arrivants: A New World Trilogy*. (London: Oxford UP, 1981): 10. All subsequent page references are to this edition and appear in the text. *The Arrivants* combines the separately issued volumes *Rights of Passage* (1967), *Masks* (1968), and *Islands* (1969).

Cortez to come. (p. 10)

The voice reveals the pain of parting, a condition arising from the forced separation of man from his environment:

> It will be a long time before we see
> this land again, these trees
> again, drifting inland with the sound
> of surf, smoke rising
>
> It will be a long time before we see
> these farms again, soft wet slow green
> again; Aburi, Akwamu,
> mist rising (p. 11)

In most of the poems in *Rights of Passage*, Brathwaite employs a poetic figure designated "Tom". As a representative of the old generation of African-Caribbeans, Tom stands as the link between the African past and the New World of the Caribbean and by extension, America. He is therefore a more credible voice for the exploration of the violent history of slavery, the suffering of the Blacks in the diaspora, and the desire of the Black man to assert his racial origin. As we learn from Tom, diaspora experience amounts to cultural void and losses. Grey memories of the horror of Black experience emerge in Tom's grieving voice:

> for we who have achieved nothing
> work
> who have built
> dream
> who have forgotten all
> dance
> and dare to remember
> the paths we shall never remember
> again: Atumpa talking and the harvest branch-
> es, all the tribes of Ashanti dreaming the dream
> of Tutu, Anokye and the Golden Stool, built
> in Heaven for our nation by the work
> of lightning and the brilliant adze: and now nothing (p. 13)

In "Tom", the poem just quoted, Brathwaite records cultural discontinuity and the decay of values as the realities of the Black man's experience. The reference to the Ashanti art (of the Golden Stool) signifies the glory of the past, which is lost in the New World. The feeling of emptiness (material and spiritual) is amplified through the repetition of the word "nothing" and the choice of a visually lean pattern of lineation:

> nothing
> so let me sing
> nothing
> now
> let me remember
> nothing
> now
>
> let me suffer
> nothing
> to remind me now
> of my lost children (p. 13)

In "Postlude/Home", the sense of cultural uprootedness evokes an inner search for racial origin. The voice here is more active and more critical than Tom, whose fatalism shows in the obsession with memories of the past. The voice in "Postlude/Home" adopts a more rational strategy for dealing with the problems around him. First, he descends into his innermost self to meditate on the cardinal questions that define the life of the Black Caribbean. Second, he rejects the non-committal passivity of Tom, dismissing his historical excursion as evidence of the "unflamed remains" (p. 78) of a wasted generation. The questions of racial origin, colour, alienation and exploitation in the New World are identified as grave problems needing urgent solution. Brathwaite records these subjects as emblems of the marginalization and exclusion of a race. The atmosphere of insecurity and disorientation compounds the crisis of identity:

> Where then is the nigger's
> home?
> In Paris Brixton Kingston
> Rome?
> Here?
> Or in Heaven? (p. 77)

The status of the African-Caribbean as an exile and the grim presence of poverty are revealed as additional burdens:

> Will exile never
> end?
> Will these spent
> tears,
> poor pauper's pence,
> earn him a little
> solace here
> bought if not given? (p. 77)

As a new voice, the speaker in "Postlude/Home" is eager to end the "loveless toil" (p. 78) and release the black race from the fettered condition of a snail chained to its shell (p. 79).

For the Black in the diaspora, the enthusiasm for homecoming, a condition motivated by physical separation from his cultural origin, often fizzles out upon real contact with Africa. The search for cultural roots in Africa, and the determination to base a newly won sense of collective Black reality upon its discovery, can thus only have meaning as an imaginative or intellectual quest. In Brathwaite's "The New Ships", for instance, the physical return to Africa brings with it serious psycho-cultural problems. The Black Caribbean returning to Africa faces alienation and crisis of identity in the very same Africa he has so passionately wished to experience:

> I tossed my net
> but the net caught
> no fish
>
> I dipped a wish
> but the well
> was dry
> (...)
> I travelled to a distant town
> I could not find my mother
> I could not find my father
> I could not hear the drum
>
> Whose ancestor am I (p. 125)

Rhetorical questions reveal the anguished state of the returning exile and define the double dislocation which history imposes on him:

> Whose
> brother, now, am I?
> could these soft huts
> have held me?
> Wattle daubed on wall,
> straw-hatted roofs (p. 126)

"The New Ships" therefore presents the Caribbean complex of the deculturalized individual, divested of the essence of racial identity and living, as Lloyd Brown puts it, the life of the "outcast archetype".[72]

---

[72] Lloyd W. Brown, "The African Heritage and the Harlem Renaissance: A Re-evaluation". *African Literature Today* 9 (1978): 4-5.

African Landscape, History and Culture

Gerald Moore identifies the physical environment as an essential subject of Black aesthetics and argues that the Black poet

> does not so much inhabit this landscape as become inhabited by it. Its rivers flow through his veins, its branches toss in his hair, its planets burn through the bone of his forehead and irradiate his skull, its volcanoes stir and grumble in his throat.[73]

The portrait of the African landscape in *The Arrivants* is part of the poet's identification with the Black world and his desire for psychic integration with this world. However, following Moore's argument about the Black poet reflecting his landscape, the style adopted in this case is not a romantic evocation but a realistic portrait of Africa, making its existing topographical and architectural features serve the purpose of signifying shifts in culture, history and human experience in general.

In *Masks*, topographical and architectural images are used to signify on the nature of African history and landscape. "Timbuctu" speaks of the "world of walls" and the surrounding "plains of dust" (p. 106). Images of ruin dominate the poems on individual ancient African cities. In "Ougadougou", the scenes of chaotic incursion prevail; we see the "red whispering walls" of advancing fire, mocking the houses and hear the sound of walls crumbling and the cries of children filled with the terror of invaders:

> The heat
> was before us; mirages danced
> in its silver; our brittle walls
> crumbled, flat walking roofs
>
> tumbled; red tongues
> licked grass from the streets,
> children screamed, women run,
> crackled sparks' eyes crashing to ashes;
> goats butted and turned, blinded; horses
> stamped. (p. 104)

In "Timbuctu", the poet laments the ruin of Africa through the mindless exploitation of its human resources. Here, the image of dust emphasizes the tragic shrinking of Africa to a wasteland:

> And what wealth here, what
> riches, when the gold returns

---

[73] Gerald Moore, "The Negro Poet and his Landscape". in Ulli Beier (ed.), *Introduction to African Literature* (London: Longman, 1979): 161.

> to dust, the walls
>
> we raised return again
> to dust; and what sharp winds,
> teeth'd with the desert's sand,
> rise in the sun's dry
>
> brilliance where our mosques
> mock ignorance, mock pride,
> burn in the crackled blaze of time,
> return again to whispers, dust. (p. 106)

Other levels of symbolic representation of landscape and history occur in *Masks*. In "Prelude", for instance, the glory of the African past is reflected in the ancient kingdoms of Songhai, Mali, Chad, Ghana, Timbuctu, Volta and Benin. However, we are quickly reminded of "the bitter wastes" which are the relics of a ruined landscape. As part of his artistic figuration of Africa, Brathwaite recalls the history of Shaka, the legendary warrior-king who, as we have mentioned in the earlier section of this study mustered the greatest and most committed army in the nineteenth century for the purpose of creating a Zulu nation. Like Wole Soyinka, Sédar Senghor and Mazisi Kunene, Brathwaite sees in Shaka the personification of the Pan-African vision.

Brathwaite treats cultural themes through the use of mythological and material codes that reflect the African world. Again, in "Prelude", he goes beyond the African landscape and history to examine the mytho-cultural elements that anchor life in Africa. One of such elements is ancestral worship. In the mode of ritual enactment, Brathwaite expresses the spiritual bond between the living and the dead. Earth is the space in which the spiritual and the terrestrial beings are linked:

> Nana Firimpong
> once you were here
> hoed the earth
> and left it for me
> green rich ready
> with yam shoots, the
> tuberous smooth of cassava (p. 91)

The sacrificial totems of ancestral rituals emerge in the poem within an invocatory context:

> take the blood of the fowl
> drink
> take the *eto*, mashed plantain,
> that my women have cooked

> eat
> and be happy
> drink
> may you rest
> for the year has come round
> again. (p. 91)

Brathwaite alludes to the regenerative essence of Asase Yaa, the Akan earth goddess:

> Asase Yaa,
> You, Mother of Earth,
> on whose soil
> I have placed my tools
> on whose soil
> I will hoe
> I will work
> the year has come round
> again;
> thirsty mouth of the dust
> is ready for water
> for seed (p. 26)

There is also an allusion to the familiar propitiatory practice, which attends the worship of the earth goddess. For this purpose, Brathwaite employs the traditional prayer rites:

> And may the year
> this year of all years
> be fruitful
> beyond the fruit of your labour:
> shoots faithful to tip
> juice to stem
> leaves to green;
>
> and may the knife
> or the cut-
> lass not cut
> me; roots blunt,
> shoots break,
> green wither (p. 92)

The drum is one of Africa's most vital cultural symbols. In "The Making of the Drum", Brathwaite describes the processes by which materials are assembled and fused to create the talking drum. The cultural relevance of this poem lies not only in its description of the production of the drum but also in its evocation of an aesthetic practice in which the drum transmits poetry.

Borrowing from the aesthetic convention in which the poet-drummer addresses the components of the drum, Brathwaite apostrophises the animal from which the skin for the drum is derived. For yielding its skin, the animal is accommodated into the aesthetic of the drum and the ritual essence that the drumming art supports. Thus, the drummer praises the animal for taking a role in Man's relation with the gods:

> Bless you, four-footed animal, who eats rope,
> skilled
> upon rocks, horned with our sin;
> stretch your skin, stretch
>
> it tight on our hope;
> we have killed
> you to make a thin
> voice that will reach
>
> further than hope
> further than heaven, that will
> reach deep down tour gods where the thin
> light cannot leak (p. 94)

The hollow wood cut from the *tweneduru* tree, like "the hollow blood/that makes a womb" (p. 95) symbolizes the re-creative essence of organic objects. The drum-maker retrieves this creative essence from the wood by connecting its essence with other objects involved in the making of the drum. Gourds and rattles are external materials of the drum. They are used to enhance the quality of the sound of the drum. Brathwaite alludes to this unity of objects in the image of the harmony of sounds, the "clash rattle, sing gourd", that "never leaves time's dancers weary" (p. 97). The gong-gong, also external to the drum, performs a ritual function that enhances man-god union:

> God is dumb
> until the drum
> speaks.
>
> The drum
> is dumb
> until the gong-gong leads
>
> it. Man made,
> the gong-gong's
> iron eyes
> of music
> walk us through the humble

dead to meet

the dumb
blind drum
where Odomankoma speaks (p. 97)

The Deployment of African Oral Aesthetics

Brathwaite's portrait of the image of Africa is made through an imaginative transfer of African aesthetic materials. Prominent among these forms are the praise tradition, ritual chants, dirges and mythology. These materials exist in the pages of *The Arrivants* as transposed elements.

It is necessary to elaborate on Brathwaite's transfer of the rhythm of drum-poetry. His investment in African aesthetic products shows in his skilful adaptation of the Akan drum-poetry genre. One must first acknowledge that the African talking drum is a versatile musical instrument that can be coaxed to speak poetry. Kwabena Nketia highlights the significance of this drum-type in his description of the typology of Akan oral poetry. Drums are used in Akan society for making announcements; and they are also a "vehicle of literature"[74]. Nketia locates the context in which the drum functions as a medium of poetic communication: "On state occasions, they drum poems of special interest to the chief and the community as a whole."[75] These poems are of various types, but fall into only four groups. One category is traditionally referred to as *Anyaneanyana*. It is typified by a standard opening formula, the addressing of the drum's components (wood, animal skin, strings), the deities, the cock, and the spirits that inhabit the Akan metaphysical realm. Other types listed by Nketia are the panegyric drum-poems, the proverb-type rendered as an independent piece or incorporated into other forms, and the more general drum-poem used for the purposes of announcement and greeting and for heralding royal appearances.

There are two examples of drum-poetry in Brathwaite's trilology. Both are of the *Anyaneanyana* type. Further information on the nature of this sub-genre of drum-poetry may help in appreciating Brathwaite's adaptation of this form. Nketia mentions the ancestor-drummer as one of the figures addressed in *Anyaneanyana*. He identifies repetition and ideophones as central aspects of the

---

[74] J.H. Kwabena Nketia, "Akan Poetry". in Ulli Beier (ed.), *Introduction to African Literature*: 29.
[75] ibid

drum-poem's internal qualities. This sub-genre also has its own closing formula, which is either "I am learning/Let me succeed" or "I am addressing you/And you will understand". Some of the vital elements of Akan drum-poetry are adaptively demonstrated in "The Awakening", which opens with an invocation to Asase Yaa:

> Asase Yaa, Earth,
> if I am going away now,
> you must help me. (p. 156)

The ancestor-drummer is also apostrophised in the poet's search for poetic illumination:

> Divine Drummer,
> 'Kyerema,
> if time sends me
> walking that dark
> path again, you
> must help me.
> If I sleep,
>
> you must knock me
> awake... (p. 156)

As we find in the chapters on Osundare, Mapanje and Udechukwu, the cock symbol occurs in Brathwaite's poetry to represent the passage of time. In Brathwaite's adaptation, the cock is an icon in the awakening archetype:

> I will rise
> and stand on my feet
>
> slowly slowly
> ever so slowly
>
> I will rise
> and stand on my feet.
>
> Like akoko the cock
> like akoko the cock
>
> who cries
> in the early dawn
>
> akoko bon 'opa
> akoko tua bon (pp. 156-157)

Using the typical closing formula of *Anyaneanyana*, Brathwaite ends:

121

> I am learning
> let me succeed
>
> I am learning
> let me succeed... (p. 157)

Other features of drum-poetry are shown in "Atumpa", where repetition of sound is reflected as the opening formula of drum-produced poetry. For instance, "Atumpa" opens with the lines: *"kon kon kon kon/kun kun kun kun"* (p. 98). These ideophones represent the sound of the drum. The poet also borrows the more extensive phrasal repetition type which the drum-poet employs to add sound quality to his art:

> Odomankoma 'Kyerema says
> Odomankoma 'Kyerema says
> The great drummer of Odomankoma says
> The great drummer of Odomankoma says
>
> that he has come from sleep
> that he has come from sleep
> and is arising
> and is arising
>
> like akoko the cock
> like akoko the cock
> who crows in the morning
> who crows in the morning (pp. 98-99)

Kwesi Yankah notes that there are ritual observances associated with the talking drum. The drummer's address to the spirit who inhabits the wood that yields the drum's wooden component is an essential ritual practice. Yankah explains the reason for this practice:

> The wood of the talking drum being regarded as a spirit, the carver of the drum often performs a series of rituals before and after they have been carved. And the talking drummer himself, aware of the vindictive spirit of the materials out of which the drum is made, often drums their praise appellations (hardly verbalised) in a dawn broadcast, and prays to them not to interfere with his drumming.[76]

Brathwaite registers this mytho-aesthetic practice in "Atumpa" through the invocation of the tree spirit:

> Funtumi Akora
> Tweneboa Akora

---

[76] Kwesi Yankah, "Voicing and Drumming the Poetry of Praise: The Case for Aural Literature". in Kofi Anyidoho, *et al* (eds.), *Interdisciplinary Dimensions of African Literature* (Washington DC: Three Continents, 1985): 149.

> Spirit of the Cedar
> Spirit of the Cedar Tree
> Twenebou Kodia (p. 98)

The significance of "The Awakening" and "Atumpan" is that they help to reflect a poet's re-discovery of his origin and to express, through reduplicative, echoic and transformative representation of the sound-universe of the drums, his desire for psychic re-unification with African aesthetic tradition.

Recitative praise poetry which, as Ruth Finnegan states, is a more extensive evocation of a hero's exploits,[77] forms part of the resources in Brathwaite's recast of the African oral aesthetics. Used to great effect in the Ghanaian *apae*, which Yankah describes as

> poetry recited for the chief as he sits in state on occasions of *durbar*. It consists essentially of the chief's strong appellations, but the chief's appellations are generally not conveyed in *apae* alone.[78]

Yankah goes further:

> With a sword in his right hand, the *apae* performer (*obrafo*) gesticulates and mimes, makes faces, and forms such facial configurations as would depict the mood of the poem he recites. In some Akan areas, such as Denkyira where *apae* was performed for my recording, reciters put on a special robe, which according to the *abrafo*, puts them in a different world.[79]

In "Tutu", a poem laden with what Daniel Kunene calls "praise reference names"[80], Brathwaite reworks the poetic mode of *apae* to present the royal image of the Osei Tutu, the Ashanti King. The poem starts with the typical *apae* heraldic formula and directs the audience to the rich paraphernalia of Osei Tutu, the ancestral symbol of the Ashanti nation:

> see the bright symbols he's clothed himself in:
> gold, that the sun may continue to shine
>
> bringing wealth and warmth to the nation;
> mirrors of brass to confound the blind
>
> darkness; calico cloth to keep us from sin. (p. 141)

Praise names such as "Atakora Firimpong" and images such as "the lions", "cracker of iron" and "black rock where the battle axe sings" are used in

---

[77] Ruth Finnegan, *Oral Poetry: Its Nature, Significance and Social Context*. (London: Cambridge UP, 1977): 12.

[78] Kwesi Yankah, "To Praise or Not to Praise the King: The Akan *Apae* in the Context of Referential Poetry". *Research in African Literatures* 14, 3 (Fall 1983): 384.

[79] ibid: 387.

[80] Daniel P. Kunene, *Heroic Poetry of the Basotho* (London: Oxford UP, 1971)

reflecting the king's might. Tutu's invincibility is also underlined by images, which associate him with mystical phenomena:

> Whispers of dark
> sasabonsam of darkness
>
> will forever fear
> his black rings of iron.
>
> the rings
> spiked with thorn (p. 142)

In Brathwaite's poetry, the incorporation of the Ogun-Xango archetype of creativity and violence is one of the most enduring attempts at re-creating the African mythology in order to understand the past and to reflect a New World vision. In doing this, poetic figures are associated with Ogun-Xango essences. This technique of reconstructing mythology in the context of contemporary experiences is located in Gordon Rohlehr's association of Ogun with Tom who undergoes "the process of discovering their own submerged spirit."[81]

Brathwaite's "Ogun" explores the creative archetype, what Louis James describes as the "assertion of the secret god-carver."[82] The speaker tells of Tom's creative skill, the essence he shares with Ogun:

> My uncle made chairs, tables, balanced doors on, dug out
> coffins, smoothing the white wood out
>
> With plane and quick sandpaper until
> it shone like his short-sighted glasses. (p. 242)

Like Ogun, Tom is associated with metal and his creative method is that in which metal objects are fused:

> The knuckles of his hands were sil-
> vered knobs of nails hit, hurt and flat-
> tened out with blast of heavy hammer. (p. 242)

We watch the carver's "saw teeth" (p. 242) on mahogany, his knife on "a block of wood" (p. 243) and then as he cuts, he hears "the creak of forests" (p. 243). These images of metal acting on wood thus reveal the paradox of creation

---

[81] Gordon Rohlehr, "The Rehumanization of History: Regeneration of Spirit: Apocalypse and Revolution in Brathwaite's *The Arrivants* and *X/Self*". in Stewart Brown (ed.), *The Art of Kamau Brathwaite* (Middamorgan: Seren, 1995): 199.

[82] Louis James, "Brathwaite and Jazz". in Stewart Brown (ed.), *The Art of Kamau Brathwaite* (Middamorgan: Seren, 1995): 68.

by destruction. New creation is described in the images of an object that gathers life:

> cutting his way
> along its yellow whorls until his hands could feel
>
> how it had swelled and shivered, breathing air,
> its weathered green burning to rings of time,
>
> its contoured grain still tuned to roots and water. (p. 243)

There is a different form of creation made to reflect the destructive capacity of nature and the violent side of the god-carver:

> And as he worked within his
> shattered
> Sunday shop, the wood took shape: dry shuttered
>
> eyes, slack anciently everted lips, flat
> ruined face, eaten by pox, ravaged by rat
>
> and woodworm, dry cistern mouth, cracked
> gullet crying for the desert, the heavy black
>
> enduring jaw; lost pain, lost iron;
> emerging woodwork image of his anger. (p. 243)

This violence is linked with the merger of the two essences of Ogun and Xango, a process which Rohlehr says embodies "the two sides of Apocalypse: destructive/recriminatory and creative/renascent."[83] The Ogun-Xango coalition is represented symbolically in the poem as the fusion of iron and fire, the "blue high-tensioned cables" (p. 243) or the "black rigid thunder he had never heard within his hammer" (p. 243). As we have mentioned much earlier in this study, the battle between Ogun and Sango in Soyinka's *Idanre* represents this fusion.

In traditional African society, the dirge form is a distinctive verbal art that defines the relationship between the living and the dead. In the Akan community, a setting from which Brathwaite makes much of his aesthetic transfer, the dirge is an essential constituent of the rites of passage. In the chapter on Anyidoho, we have already seen the ways in which the dirge form could be manipulated to comment on society. Brathwaite's "Tano" is an improvised Akan dirge, which contains typical dirge patterns such as the wailing

---

[83] Gordon Rohlehr, "The Rehumanization of History: Regeneration of Spirit: Apocalypse and Revolution in Brathwaite's *The Arrivants* and *X/Self*": 197.

tone, reference to the dead, and address to the supernatural force. The poem begins with a long, wailing tone conveyed by breaking down the set condolatory phrase *damirifa due* into its sound-constituents. The dirge itself is rendered within the frame of an invocation to Tano, the Akan river-god. The poem is, however, more than a dirge, for like Oculi's *Orphan*, it captures the orphan complex in a poet who laments the cultural deracination of his own personality. Also, like Okigbo, who returns from exile to his ancestral roots in "Idoto" via a union with the spiritual essence of the sacred river, Brathwaite invokes Tano for protection and guidance:

> Exiled from here
>
> to seas
> of bitter edges,
>
> whips of white worlds,
> stains of new
>
> rivers,
> I have returned
> to you. (p. 153)

The ancestral and animist vision in Brathwaite's poetry is sustained through ritual chants and elegiac formulae. In "Masks" for instance, the structure of the traditional invocation is transposed imaginatively. Following the traditional structure of ritual chant, the poet starts with the conventional introductory salute to the deities:

> God of the path-
> way,
> God of the
> tree,
> God of all part-
> ing, we
> greet you. (p. 130)

Again, like Okigbo, Brathwaite laments the attrition of the values once placed on the African deities, which are the symbols of Black cultural heritage. The elegiac rhythm of "Masks" is particularly suitable for the depiction of the decay of this heritage.

Thus, in relating with the African muse, Brathwaite also maintains aesthetic links with African artists. This "manifestation of Africa in the New

World"[84] occurs in the form of recreating the mask symbol. As we have seen in "Masks", Brathwaite draws on the Ogun mythology again, reflecting those icons associated with the deity. The Ogun-Xango fusion, which we find in "Ogun", recurs in "Masks" and this manifests in images of axe and lightning (iron and fire) expressing violence ("your tree/has been split/by a white axe/of lightning" p. 130) and also creative vision (hearts/rustle their secrets" p. 131).

---

[84] Mervyn Morris, "Overlapping Journeys: *The Arrivants*". in Stewart Brown (ed.), *The Art of Kamau Brathwaite* (Middamorgan: Seren, 1995): 121.

CONCLUSION: LINKAGES AND THE READING ARENA

As it appears, the various poets studied here are connected in terms of their vision of the Black world and relation with oral traditions. As we have also seen, Africa is the landscape upon which almost all of them set their art in reflecting the Black World. In Osundare's poetry for instance, what we find is an art, which gives voice to those who have been manipulated and silenced by the so-called dominant class. By reflecting the society through the experiences of the underprivileged majority, Osundare extends the debate on the vexed question of the social responsibility of rulers in Africa. In this sense, there is a thematic link between *The Eye of the Earth* in which the African experience is constructed from the perspective of the dialectics of mode of production[85] and *Waiting Laughters*, which expresses a sense of hope.[86] This is related to the kind of vision, which Oculi expresses in both *Orphan* and *Malak*. As we have argued, Oculi uses these texts to make a broad interpretation of the African experience. For him, the orphan concept embodies a symbolic connection between the orphan status and contemporary Africa that has been disconnected from its own essence.

As we have seen, Soyinka incorporates the myth of Ogun and the legend of Shaka in *Idanre* and *Ogun Abibiman* as revolutionary archetypes in the course of shaping the destiny of the Black race. Of course, this kind of vision is also reflected in his *Mandela's Earth and Other Poems* where Nelson Mandela, the South African hero of the struggle against apartheid becomes the contemporary extension of the Ogun-Shaka revolutionary archetype.[87] In interpreting Soyinka's vision of the Black world, the ways in which titles and prefaces are constituted are as important as the contents of the works. Soyinka's choice of the Akan word "Abibiman" for his *Ogun Abibiman* is significant for revealing the Black consciousness. As Soyinka himself says, the word, means in Akan"The Black Nation; the land of the Black Peoples; the Black World; that which

---

[85] See Charles Bodunde, "Niyi Osundare and the Materialist Vision: A Study of *The Eye of the Earth*" *Ufahamu* XXV. II (Spring 1997): 81-100.

[86] See also, Charles Bodunde, "Political Forces and Socio-Aesthetic Phenomena in Niyi Osundare's *Waiting Laughters*". *Commonwealth: Essays and Studies* 21, 2 (Spring 1999): 19-27.

[87] See Charles Bodunde, "Tributes, Censures and Transitions: Soyinka's *Mandela's Earth and Other Poems*". *Wasafiri* 14, (Autumn 1991): 2-6.

pertains to, the matter, the affair of, Black peoples."[88] True leadership is therefore defined in the context of actions meant to concretely represent and advance this world. Also in the preface to *Ogun Abibiman*, Soyinka takes Samora Machel's 1976 declaration of struggle against Rhodesia as an inspiring act that ignites "a people's collective will."[89]

A similar pattern of imaging Africa reflects in Brathwaite's *The Arrivants*, where the African landscape shows in the portrait of Africa's old kingdoms and cities. As we have observed earlier, Brathwaite's artistic interpretation of the history of Africa connects other aesthetic recasts, particularly the pan-African symbolization in the works of Soyinka, Kunene and Senghor.

As the study shows, remarkable links exist among the Black poets in the way in which they approach oral traditions even when their individual regional (even cultural) bases appear to separate them. For instance, Osundare borrows from the Yoruba oral traditions and Ojaide reflects Urhobo aesthetics in his poetry. However, the two poets have a common pursuit in their use of the Iroko (tree) icon as a means of articulating their criticism of a political formation in which the ordinary people are crippled by the powerful minority. This form of link is also exemplified in the ways in which some of the poets recast the dirge genre. The discussion has shown how the traditional funeral dirge serves as a source of link between the works of Anyidoho, Ojaide, Udechukwu and Oculi where the genre functions as the instrument of reflecting the paradox of renewal of hope and life within the atmosphere of death and decay. In this regard, the closest connection is between Anyidoho's image of life-in-death and Udechukwu's vision of "fresh grass" and "new song" after the rain. Furthermore, the cock, which is the dominant image in rituals and folklore, provides a unifying icon for Brathwaite, Mapanje, Osundare, and Udechukwu.

With these poets, one notices the tendency to act as the public voice. In this, they adopt the voice of the traditional minstrel whose art is an expression of the people's social and historical experiences. Again, nearly all the poets employ the image of the ancestral mask, which represents a link with the people's past. From the discussion, Okigbo, Brathwaite and Ohaeto are shown to be particularly strong in deploying the mask symbol as a means of mediating the world around them. There is a sense in which both Anyidoho and Oculi are connected in their use of the narrative voice in poetry. Anyidoho's "Awoyo" and

---

[88] Wole Soyinka, *Ogun Abibiman*. (London: Rex Collings, 1980): 23.
[89] ibid.

Oculi's "village gossip" as we have already noted are rendered in the typical song-of-abuse mode. In both cases, characters are set in dramatic monologue and the purpose is to moralize.

As pointed out earlier, the reason why the works of these poets easily lend themselves to dramatic reading can be traced to the fact that there is a conscious attempt to incorporate performance structures into the texts. Quite a number of these poets have engaged in dramatic readings of their works and they do this to reconnect their art to the oral performance tradition from which they have borrowed. Osofisan's dramatic readings from *Dream-Seeker on Divining Chain* at the Lake Forest Library (Lake Forest) and the Live Bait Theater (Chicago) both in the United States are good examples of the ways in which a written text based on aesthetic transfer reflects its innate performance features through dramatic reading. Osofisan seized the occasion to inform the American audience about the essential image in his book: "The collection", says Osofisan, "is conceived as a divination process... there is the image of the priest who divines with Ifa [divination] chain."[90] Transcriptions from the video tapes on Osofisan's reading at the Live Bait Theater show interesting relations between poet and audience and the poet's attempt to situate his poetry within a performance atmosphere which embraces singing, chanting and drumming. At the beginning of his reading on 28th February 1993, at the Lake Forest Library, Osofisan told the audience: "I need a number of voices to join me and some drummers... I am going to ask you to sing with me sometimes". Also at the Live Bait Theater, he told the audience:

> Copies of the poems [to be read] have been distributed to you and I am going to ask you to participate with me when I get to that section. Meanwhile you're going to sing a refrain with me... [sings the song]

In performing the poem "Exultation", Osofisan again requested that the audience should participate:

> In this next poem, you're going to read with me... [He tries a drum]. Unfortunately this drum is not good. This is not a drum at all. [laughter from the audience] This drum can't do anything ... [more laughter from the audience]. How do I handle this drum? [He tries the drum again] The drum has just one voice ... We better forget the drum. The essential thing is that I sing and you respond.

---

[90] Femi Osofisan speaking about his poetry on 24th February, 1993 at Live Bait Theater, Chicago, USA. Quotations relating to Osofisan's reading are transcriptions from the video tapes produced by the Ragdale Foundation, Lake Forest, USA. The Ragdale Foundation offered Osofisan and two other African writers a Creative Writing Fellowship in 1993 and arranged a series of public readings including Osofisan's presentation at the Live Bait Theater.

The poem is in two voices. The male voice reads the line in normal print and the female voice the other... [while he audience reads, Osofisan sings to the reading].

At the end, the whole experience is a dialogic interplay between the poet and the audience.

Anyidoho and Brathwaite are also associated with this form of dramatic rendering of poetry. For Anyidoho, the essence of performance poetry lies in engaging poet and audience in dialogue:

> Drawing on the popular African tradition of call-and-response, the performer may even establish a pattern that makes all allowances for audience participation. One of the most important implications of this orientation towards a poetry meant for performance is the manner in which the actual process of writing may be influenced by the awareness of a potential audience presence and participation. In my poem "Fertility Game", for example, provision is made for co-opting the audience into the performance with the line "Come back home, Agbenoxevi, come back home". This phrase is to be repeated at carefully marked intervals sometimes signalled by an appropriate gesture or some voice indicator.[91]

Anyidoho gives a brief review of Brathwaite's performance of his poems during a tour of Ghana and refers to Zagba Oyortey's comment that

> Brathwaite offered the audience a rare insight into the nature of oral performance as it obtains in Africa and the Caribbean. He used a combination of percussive African words, "Dam...Damirifa...Due" [an Akan dirge-chant], as a spring board from which he sprung to bring out the history of the Caribbean through reggae and dub rhythms seen as typifying the socially responsive and communicative role of art [or poetry in this case], which reaches beyond its individual voice to encapsulate and amplify popular aspirations.[92]

Most often, it is the oral medium, which attracts the audience and as Udechukwu argues, speaking of his own poetry, traditional chants and songs help to engage audience participation no matter their cultural background:

> We went to this conference in Iserlohn [Germany] three days ago and at the opening of my exhibition on Saturday, I read from my poems and before I started, I did about two minutes of singing and chanting from oral traditions and that was what people there at the exhibition remembered more than any thing even though they couldn't understand the language because I was singing and chanting in Igbo. They could respond to the rhythm and even the modulation of voice ... They were just enthralled. You could see that from their faces. I think the oral tradition is something to explore seriously.[93]

---

[91] Kofi Anyidoho, "Poetry as Dramatic Performance: The Ghanaian Experience". *Research in African Literatures* 22, 2 (Summer 1991): 47.
[92] Cited in Kofi Anyidoho, "Poetry as Dramatic Performance: The Ghanaian Experience".: 46.
[93] Charles Bodunde, "Interview with Obiora Udechukwu". *Tape Recording* 18th January, 1999, Bayreuth, Germany.

Finally, with the poets studied, one discovers that aesthetic transfer allows for a more articulate presentation of vision and in a more fundamental sense, it is a reliable mode of establishing linkages between one poet and the other and between poets and their audiences.

BIBLIOGRAPHY

Primary Sources

Achebe, Chinua & Dubem Okafor (eds.). *Don't Let Him Die.* Enugu: Fourth Dimension Publishers, 1970.

Anyidoho, Kofi. *A Harvest of our Dreams.* London: Heinemann, 1984.

Anyidoho, et al (eds.). *The Fate of Vultures: New Poetry from Africa.* London: Heinemann, 1989.

Brathwaite, Kamau. *The Arrivants: A New World Trilogy.* London: Oxford University Press, 1981.

Ezenwa-Ohaeto. *The Voice of the Night Masquerade.* Ibadan: Kraft Books, 1996.

Fourie, Pieter. *Shaka.* Cape Town: Longman, 1976.

Kiguli, Susan. *The African Saga.* Kampala: Femrite Publications, 1998.

Kunene, Mazisi. *Emperor Shaka the Great.* London: Heinemann, 1979.

Launko, Okinba. *Dream-Seeker on Divining Chain.* Ibadan: Kraft Books, 1993.

Mapanje, Jack. *Of Chameleons and the Gods.* London: Heinemann, 1983.

Mapanje, Jack & Landeg, White. *Oral Poetry from Africa.* New York: Longman, 1983.

Mofolo, Thomas. *Chaka: An Historical Romance.* (Trans., F.H. Dutton) London: Oxford University Press, 1971.

Oculi, Okello. *Orphan.* Nairobi: East African Publishing House, 1968.

---. *Malak.* Nairobi: East African Publishing House, 1976.

Ojaide, Tanure. *The Fate of Vultures and Other Poems.* Lagos: Malthouse Press Ltd., 1990.

---. *Delta Blues & Home Songs.* Ibadan: Kraft Books, 1997.

---. *Invoking the Warrior.* Spirit Ibadan: Heinemann, 1998.

Osundare, Niyi. *Village Voices.* Ibadan: Evans Brothers Ltd., 1984.

---. *Songs of the Marketplace.* Ibadan: New Horn Press, 1987.

---. *Waiting Laughters*. Lagos: Malthouse Press Ltd., 1990.

p'Bitek, Okot. *Song of Lawino & Song of Ocol*. London: Heinemann, 1984.

Read, John & Clive, Wake. *Senghor: Prose and Poetry*. London: Heinemann, 1979.

Soyinka, Wole. *A Dance of the Forests*. London: Oxford University Press, 1963.

---. *Idanre and Other Poems*. London: Methuen, 1967.

---. *Ogun Abibiman*. London: Rex Collings, 1976.

Udechukwu, Obiora. *What the Madman Said*. Bayreuth: Boomerang Press, 1990.

Secondary Sources

Interviews

Bodunde, Charles. "Interview with Odia Ofeimun" 27th November 1993, Ilorin, Nigeria.

---. "Interview with Femi Osofisan" 12th March 1994, Ibadan, Nigeria.

---. "Interview with Niyi Osundare" 12th September 1994, Ibadan, Nigeria.

---. "Interview with Obiora Udechukwu" 18th January 1999, Bayreuth, Germany.

---. "Interview with Tanure Ojaide" 12th March 1999, Fez, Morocco.

---. "Interview with Nduka Otiono" 12th March 1999, Fez, Morocco.

---. "Interview with Okello Oculi" 13th March 1999, Fez, Morocco.

---. "Interview with Kofi Anyidoho" 26th March 1999, Fez, Morocco.

---. "Interview with Ogaga Ifowodo" 26th March 1999, Bayreuth, Germany.

---. "Interview with Uche Nduka" 26th March 1999, Bayreuth, Germany.

---. "Interview with Deena Padayachee" 9th April 1999, Tubingen, Germany.

---. "Telephone Interview with Toyin Adewale" 27th May 1999, Bayreuth, Germany.

---. "Interview with Susan Kiguli" 28th October 1999, Bayreuth, Germany.

Rowell, H. Charles. "Interview with Aimé Césaire" *Callalo: Journal of Afro-American and African Arts* 12. 38 (1989).

Wilkinson, Jane. *Talking with African Writers: Interviews*. London: James Currey, 1992.

Articles, Books Conference papers and Dissertations

Abarry, Abu. "Oral Rhetoric and Poetics". S. O. Asein (ed.), *Comparative Approaches to Modern African Literature*. Ibadan: Department of English, 1984.

Abimbola, Wande. *Sixteen Great Poems of Ifa*. New York: UNESCO, 1975.

---. *Ifa Divination Poetry*. Lagos: NOK Publisher, 1977.

Abiodun, Rowland. "The Future of African Art Studies: An African Perspective". Paper presented at the symposium of the National Museum of African Art, Washington DC, National Museum of African Art, 1990.

Adams, Lois. "The Prison and the Post-prison Writing of Wole Soyinka". PhD dissertation, University of Wisconsin, Madison, 1980.

Adedeji, Joel. "Oral Tradition and the Contemporary Theatre in Nigeria". *Research in African Literatures* 2, 2 (1971).

Ajuwon, Bade. *Funeral Dirges of Yoruba Hunters*. Lagos: NOK Publishers International, 1982.

Anyidoho, Kofi. "Kofi Awoonor and the Ewe Tradition of Songs of Abuse". in Lamuel Johnson, et al (eds.), *Toward Defining the African Aesthetic* (Washington DC: Three Continents Press, 1982).

---. "Poetry as Dramatic Performance: The Ghanaian Experience" *Research in African Literatures* 22.2 (Summer 1991).

Awoonor, Kofi. "A Study of the Influences of Oral Literature on the Contemporary Literature of Africa". PhD dissertation, State University of New York, 1972.

Babalola, S. A. *The Content and Form of Yoruba Ijala*. London: Oxford University Press, 1966.

Babalola, Adebayo. "The Traditional Poetry of Yoruba Hunters". in Ulli Beier (ed.), *Introduction to African Literature*. London: Longman, 1979.

Baker Jr., Houston. "On the Criticism of Black American Literature: One View of the Black Aesthetic". *Cornell University African Studies and Research Center Monograph Series*, 4 (1976).

Bamikunle, Aderemi. "Niyi Osundare's Poetry and the Yoruba Oral Artistic Tradition". *African Literature Today* 18 (1992).

Bascom, William. "Four Functions of Folklore". *Journal of American Folklore* 67. 226 (1954).

Beier, Ulli. "Reactions to 'Siren Limits' ". *Black Orpheus* 12 (1963).

Binns, C. T. *The Last Zulu King*. London: Longmans, Green & Co. Ltd., 1963.

Bodunde, Charles. "Tributes, Censures and Transitions: Soyinka's *Mandela's Earth and Other Poems*". *Wasafiri* 14 (Autumn 1991).

---. "Review of *The Fate of Vultures: New Poetry from Africa*". *Research in African Literatures* 22. 3 (Fall 1991).

---. "Niyi Osundare and the Materialist Vision: A Study of *The Eye of the Earth*". *Ufahamu* XXX. II (Spring 1997).

---. "Political Forces and Socio-Aesthetic Phenomena in Niyi Osundare's *Waiting Laughters*". *Commonwealth: Essays and Studies* 21. 2 (Spring 1999).

Brathwaite, Kamau. "The Love axe (1): Developing a Caribbean Aesthetic 1962-1974". *African Studies and Research Center Monograph Series* 4 (1996).

Brown, Lloyd .W. "The African Heritage and the Harlem Renaissance: A Re-evaluation". *African Literature Today* 9 (1978).

Chinweizu *et al*. *Toward the Decolonization of African Literature*. Enugu: Fourth Dimension, 1980.

Chukwuma, Helen. "The Oral Nature of Traditional Poetry and Language". *Journal of the Nigerian English Studies* 8. 1 (May 1976).

Deosaran, Ramesh. "Some Issues in Multiculturalism: The Case of Trinidad Tobago in the Post-Colonial Era". *Caribbean Quarterly* 33. *1* (March-June 1982).

Ebeogu, Afam. "From *Idanre* to *Ogun Abibiman*: An Examination of Soyinka's use of Ogun Image". *Journal of Commonwealth Literature* 15. 1 (August 1989).

Echeruo, M. J. "Traditional and Borrowed Elements in Nigerian Poetry". *Nigerian Magazine* 89 (June 1996).

Egudu, Romanus. "Defence of Culture in the Poetry of Christopher Okigbo". *African Literature Today* 6 (1973).

Egudu, N. Romanus. *African Poetry of the Living Dead: Igbo Masquerade Poetry*. Lewiston: The Edwin Mellen Press, 1992.

Ezenwa-Ohaeto. "Survival Strategies and the New Life of Orality in Nigerian and Ghanaian Poetry: Osundare's *Waiting Laughters* and Anyidoho's *Earthchild*." *Research in African Literatures* 22, 27 (Summer 1996).

---. *Contemporary Nigerian Poetry and the Poetics of Orality*. Bayreuth: Bayreuth African Studies, 1998.

Finnegan, Ruth. *Oral Literature in Africa*. Oxford: Clarendon Press, 1970.

---. *Oral Poetry: Its Nature, Significance and Social Context*. London: Cambridge University Press, 1977.

Furay, Michael. "Africa in Negro American Poetry to 1929". *African Literature Today* 1-4 (1972).

Gayton, A. H. "Perspectives in Folklore". *Journal of American Folklore* 64 (1951).

Gilroy, Beryl. "The Oral Culture-Effects and Expression". *Wasafiri* 22 (Autumn 1995).

Heron, George. *The Poetry of Okot p'Bitek*. London: Heinemann, 1976.

Izevbaye, Dan. "Okigbo's Portrait of the Artist as a Sunbird: A reading of Heavensgate". *African Literature Today* 6 (1973).

James, Louis "Brathwaite and Jazz". in Stewart Brown (ed.), *The Art of Kamau Brathwaite*. Middamorgan: Seren, 1995.

Jeyifo, Biodun. "What is the Will of Ogun?". in Yemi Ogunbiyi (ed.), *Perspectives on Nigerian Literature*. Lagos: Guardian Books Ltd., 1988.

Johnson, Lamuel *et al* (ed.) *Toward Defining the African Aesthetic*. Washington DC: Three Continents Press, 1982.

Kesby, D. John. "African Legends". in Richard Cavendish (ed.) *Legends of the World*. London: Orbits Publishing Ltd., 1982.

Kunene, Daniel. *Heroic Poetry of the Basotho*. London: Oxford University Press, 1971.

---. "The Crusading Writer, his Modes, Themes and Styles". in Mineke Schipper-de Leeuw (ed.), *Text and Context: Methodological Exploration in the Field of African Literature*. Leiden: African Studies Centrum, 1976.

Kunene, Mazisi. "The Relevance of African Cosmological Systems to African Literature Today". *African Literature Today* 11 (1980).

Macebuh, Stanley. "African Aesthetics in Traditional African Art". *Okike* 5 (1974).

Moore, Gerald. "The Negro Poet and his Landscape". in Ulli Beier (ed.), *Introduction to African Literature.* London: Longman, 1979.

Morris, Mervyn. "Overlapping Journeys: *The Arrivants*". in Stewart Brown (ed.), *The Art of Kamau Brathwaite.* Middamorgan: Seren, 1995.

Muller, C. F. J. *Five Hundred Years: A History of South Africa.* Pretoria: H & R Academics, 1971.

Nichol, Davidson. "The African and the Jewish Diasporas: A Comparative Study". *Présence Africaine* 114 (1980).

Nketia, Kwabena. "Akan Poetry". in Ulli Beier (ed.), *Introduction to African Literature* London: Longman, 1979.

Nwoga, Donatus. "Modern African Poetry: The Domestication of a Tradition". *African Literature Today* 10 (1979).

Obafemi, Olu. *Contemporary Nigerian Theatre - Cultural Heritage and Social Vision.* Bayreuth: Bayreuth African Studies 40, 1996.

Obichere, Boniface (ed.). *Journal of African Studies.* 12. 2 (1985).

Obiechina, E. N. "Cultural Nationalism in Modern African Creative Literature". *African Literature Today* 1-4 (1972).

Ogede, Ode. "Oral Echoes in Armah's Short Stories". *African Literature Today* 18 (1992).

Ojaide, Tanure. *Poetic Imagination in Black Africa: Essays on African Poetry.* Durham: Carolina Academic Press, 1996.

Okpewho, Isidore. *The Epic in Africa.* New York: Columbia University Press, 1979.

Osofisan, Femi. "Soyinka in the Forest of a Thousand Revellers". in Yemi Ogunbiyi (ed.), *Perspectives on Nigerian Literature.* Lagos: Guardian Books Ltd., 1980.

Osundare, Niyi. "Bard of the Tabloid Platform: A Personal Experience of Newspaper Poetry in Nigeria". Paper presented at the Canadian Association of African Studies Conference, Edmonton, Alberta, Canada, 1987.

---. "Freedom and the Creative Space". *ALA Bulletin* 24. 2 (Spring 1998).

Raum, O. F. *Chaga Childhood: A Description of Indigenous Education in an East African Tribe*. London: Oxford University Press, 1940.

Ridehalgh, Anna. "Some Recent Francophone Versions of the Shaka Story". *Research in African Literatures* 22. 2 (1991).

Roberts, Brian. *The Zulu Kings*. New York: Charles Scribner's sons, 1974.

Rohlehr, Gordon. "The Rehumanization of History: Regeneration of Spirit: Apocalypse and Revolution in Brathwaite's *The Arrivants* and *X/Self* ". in Stewart Brown (ed.), *The Art of Kamau Brathwaite*. Middamorgan: Seren, 1995.

Roscoe, Adrian. *Uhuru's Fire*. London: Cambridge University Press, 1977.

Scheub, Harold. "Review of *African Oral Traditions and Literature*". *The African Studies Review* 28. 2/3 (June/September 1985).

---. *The Tongue is Fire: South African Storytellers and Apartheid*. Madison: The University of Wisconsin Press, 1996.

Soyinka, Wole. *Myth, Literature and the African World*. London: Cambridge University Press, 1978.

Troup, Freda. *South Africa: An Historical Introduction*. London: Eyre Methuen, 1972.

Worger, William. "Clothing Dry Bones: The myth of Shaka". *Journal of African Studies* 3 (1989).

Yankah, Kwesi. "To Praise or Not to Praise the King: The Akan *Apae* in the Context of Referential Poetry". *Research in African Literatures* 14. 3 (Fall 1983).

---. "Voicing and Drumming the Poetry of Praise: The Case for Aural Literature". in Kofi Anyidoho (ed.), *Interdisciplinary Dimension of African Literature*. Washington DC: Three Continents, 1985.

INDEX

Abarry, Abu 12
Abimbola, Wande 17, 27-8, 33, 35, 39
Abiodun, Rowland 33
Achebe, Chinua 16, 91
Acholi 8-11
Adams, Lois 17
Adedeji, Joel 1
Ajuwon, Bade 44
Akan 118, 120-21, 123, 125-26, 128, 131, 138-39
Anyidoho, Kofi 3-5, 7, 63-72, 76, 89, 122, 125, 129, 131
   A Harvest of Our Dreams 63-4, 68, 71, 133
   Earth Child 70, 137
Ashanti 110, 113, 123
Awoonor, Kofi 4, 63
Babalola, S. A. 14, 17
Baker Jr., Houston 111
Bamikunle, Aderemi 43
Bascom, William 2
Beier, Ulli 16-7, 116, 120
Binns, C. T. 21
Bodunde, Charles 4, 48, 56, 61, 69, 81, 88, 91, 99, 105, 128, 131
Brathwaite, Kamau 6-7, 110, 112-15, 117-127, 129, 131
   The Arrivants: A New World 6, 112, 116, 120, 124-25, 127, 129, 133, 138-39
   Rights of Passage 112
   Islands 112
   Masks 112
Brown, Lloyd 115
Césaire, Aimé 110-11, 134
Chinweizu 12
Chukwuma, Helen 14-5
Deosaran, Ramesh 111
Esu 28-9, 39
Ewe 4, 33, 63, 135
Ewe dirge 5, 15, 36, 41, 44-5, 52-3, 55, 63-5, 67-72, 79, 88-91, 93-4, 103, 120, 125-26, 129, 131
drum-poetry 120-22
Ebeogu, Afam 17
Echeruo, Michael 16
edon 99, 103, 107-09
Egudu, Romanus 13, 73-5, 77, 81-2, 85

Ezenwa-Ohaeto 5, 7, 70, 73-4, 94-5
   The Voice of the Night Masquerade 5, 73-4, 81, 83, 94, 133
Finnegan, Ruth 1, 123
Fourie, Pieter 59
Furay, Michael 110
Gayton, A. H. 2
Gilroy, Beryl 6
heroic poetry 1, 23, 123
Heron, George 8, 10
ifa 1, 5, 17, 27-35, 39, 103
Igbo 13, 39, 73, 88, 94-5, 131
Igbo masquerade poetry 73-4, 81-2, 88, 91, 137
Ijala 14, 29, 135
ivwie 99-103, 106, 109
ivwri 99, 103, 105-07, 109
Izevbaye, Dan 13
James, Louis 124
Jeyifo, Biodun 17, 47
Johnson, Lemuel 3-4
Kesby, John 21
Kiguli, Susan 50
   The African Saga 50, 133
Kunene, P. Daniel 36, 123
Kunene, Mazisi 2, 7, 17, 22-3, 103, 107, 117, 129
   Emperor Shaka the Great 22, 133
Launko, Okinba (Femi Osofisan) 5, 27, 29, 30-5
   Dream-Seeker on Divining Chain 29, 33, 130, 133
Macebuh, Stanley 1
Mapanje, Jack 5, 7, 36-8, 40-1, 43, 45-7, 52, 70, 121, 129
   Of Chameleons and the Gods 36-7, 40, 133
masquerade 5, 73-7, 79-86, 88-91, 94-6
Mattera, Don 33
minstrel 88-9, 92-3, 129
Mofolo, Thomas 22
Moore, Gerald 116
Morris, Mervyn 127
Muller, C. F. J. 21
myth 1, 2, 5, 8, 10-1, 17, 24, 26-7, 29, 29, 31, 34, 36, 41, 45-6, 59, 67-8, 76, 94, 102-3, 105-7, 109, 117, 120, 122, 124, 127-8

Négritude 25
Nichol Davidson 110
Nketia Kwabena 120
Nwoga, Donatus 48, 88
Obafemi, Olu 29
Obichere, Boniface 2
Obiechina, E. N. 111
Oculi, Okello 4, 7, 48-50, 52-7, 59, 61-2, 126, 128-29, 130
   Orphan 48-50, 52-4, 56, 59-61, 126, 128, 133
   Malak 61-2, 128, 133
Ogede, Ode 82
ogiso 99, 103-06, 109
Ogun 5, 17-21, 24-6, 29, 107, 124-25, 127-29
Ojaide, Tanure 4-7, 99-105, 107-09, 129
   The Fate of Vultures and Other Poems 99, 104-05, 133, 136
   Delta Blues & Home Songs 103, 105, 133
   Invoking the Warrior Spirit 99-100, 103, 105, 107, 133
Okafor, Dubem 16, 91
Okigbo, Christopher 5, 7-8, 12-6, 67, 76, 88-9, 91-3, 126, 129, 136-37
   Labyrinths 12-4, 91-2, 67
   Heavensgate 13, 91, 137
   Path of Thunder 12, 91
Okpewho, Isidore 17
Oriki 1, 29
Orunmila 27, 31-3, 103
Osofisan, Femi (Okinba Launko) 5, 7, 103, 130, 131
Osundare, Niyi 4-5, 7, 36-47, 70, 89, 102, 121, 128-29
   Village Voices 36-8, 42-4, 133
   Songs of the Marketplace 47, 133
   Waiting Laughters 42, 45, 70, 128, 134, 136-37

p'Bitek, Okot 5, 7-9, 10, 12, 33, 48
   Song of Lawino & Song of Ocol 8-12, 48, 134
Raum, O. F. 2
Ridehalgh, Anna 25
Roberts, Brian 21
Rohlehr, Gordon 124-25
Roscoe, Adrian 8
Rowell, Charles 110-11
Saro Wiwa, Ken 103

Scheub, Harold 1, 63-4
Senghor, Léopold Sédar 17, 22, 25-6, 110, 117, 129, 134
Shaka/ Chaka 17, 21-6, 41, 59, 117, 128
Sango/ Xango 18, 20, 31, 124-25, 127
songs 1, 4, 5, 10-1, 29, 34, 36, 41-3, 47-8, 51, 71, 73-4, 89, 92, 99, 103, 105, 131
song-of-abuse 44, 130
Soyinka, Wole 5, 7, 15, 17-20, 22, 24-6, 28, 33, 81, 107, 117, 125, 128-29
   A Dance of the Forests 134
   Idanre and Other Poems 5, 18, 134
   Ogun Abibiman 17, 25-6, 128-29, 134, 136
Troup, Freda 21
Udechukwu, Obiora 7, 81, 88-96, 129, 131
udje 4-5, 99, 103-04, 109
Urhobo 4-5, 99-100, 103, 105, 107, 129
Wilkinson, Jane 63
Worger, William 21
Yankah, Kwesi 122-23
Yoruba 14, 17, 26-30, 33, 39, 43-5, 110, 129, 135-36

RESEARCH IN AFRICAN LITERATURES

Research in African Literatures, edited by Abiola Irele, is the premier journal of African literature studies worldwide and serves as a stimulating vehicle in English for research on the oral and written literatures of Africa. Reviews of current scholarly books, often presented as review essays, are included in every number, and a forum offers readers the opportunity to respond to issues raised in articles and book reviews. It is published quarterly.

DISSIDENT ALGERIA
Danielle Marx-Scouras, Editor

ASSIA DJEBAR: RAIS, BENTALHA...A Year Later

JEAN DANIEL: Dissident Algeria

ASSIA DJEBAR: Blood Does Not Dry on the Tongue

TASSADIT YACINE: Is a Genealogy of Violence Possible?

FETHI BENSLAMA: Identity as a Cause

HAFID GAFAITI: Power, Censorship, and the Press: The Case of Postcolonial Algeria

DANIELE DJAMILA AMRANE-MINNE: Women and Politics in Algeria from the War of Independence to Our Day

BENJAMIN STORA: Women's Writing between Two Algerian Wars

JOHN ERICKSON: Translating the Untranslated: Djebar's *Le Blance de l'Algerie*

CLARISSE ZIMRA: Sounding Off the Absent Body: Inter-textual Resonances in "La Femme qui pleure" and "La Femme en morceaux"

MILDRED MORTIMER: Coming Home: Exile and Memory in Leila Sebbar's *Le Silence des rives*

BERNARD ARESU: Narrating the Tribe: Ralhid Mimouni and Dystopia

And more
Volume 30, number 3 $16.95

Subscriptions   Send orders to: Journals Division
Individuals: $38.00   Indiana University Press
Institutions: $75.00   601 N. Morton St.
Foreign surface post: $12.50   Bloomington, IN 47404 USA
Single issue shipping: $5.00 for one,   Fax: 812-855-3830   Phone: 800-842-6796
$1.00 each additional   E-mail: Journals@Indiana.Edu
                                         URL: www.indiana.edu/~iupress/journals

List of Titles

1. *The Sudan: Ethnicity and National Cohesion.* 85 pp. DM 12.-
2. *Towards African Authenticity - Language and Literary Form.* 106 pp. DM 12.-
3. *Littératures africaines francophones.* 122 pp. DM 12.-
4. *Approaches to African Identity.* 90 pp. DM 12.- (out of print)
5. *Language and Education in Africa.* 144 pp. DM 12.- (out of print)
6. *Literature and African Identity.* 126 pp. DM 12.-
7. *Drama and Theatre in Africa.* 87 pp. DM 12.-
8. *Interviews avec des écrivains africains francophones.* 95 pp. DM 12.-
9. *Perspectives on African Music.* 139 pp. DM 18.50
10. *Douala 1893 - La Revolte des esclaves mercenaires.* 96 pp. DM 12.-
11. *African and Western Legal Systems in Contact.* 89 pp. DM 12.-
12. *Three Yoruba Artists.* 93 pp. DM 12.- (out of print)
13. *Patterns of Language Knowledge and Language Use in Botswana.* 83 pp. DM 12.-
14. *Kulankula - Interviews with Writers from Malawi and Lesotho.* 75 pp. DM 12.-
15. *English in East and Central Africa I.* 97 pp. DM 12.-
16. *Essays on Music in Africa II.* 187 pp. DM 29.- (out of print)
17. *New Religious Movements and Society in Nigeria.* 82 pp. DM 12.- (out of print)
18. *Linguistics in the Service of Africa.* 95 pp. DM 12.-
19/20. *Littérature et politique en Afrique noire.* 247 pp. DM 39.-
21/22. *Yoruba Drumming. The Dùndún Tradition.* 553 pp. DM 59.-
23. *Le Champ littéraire togolais.* 200 pp. DM 29.-
24. *English in East and Central Africa II.* 113 pp. DM 15.-
25. *Akin Euba - An Introduction to a Nigerian Composer.* 112 pp. DM 19.80
26. *Focus on Women in Africa.* 204 pp. DM 29.-
27. *Survey of Zimbabwean Writers. Educational and Literary Careers.* 172 pp. DM 29.-
28. *Koloniale Konflikte im Alltag.* 184 pp. DM 29.90
29. *Intercultural Music.* 268 pp. DM 39.-
30. *Anglophone Cameroon Writing.* 204 pp. DM 29.-
31. *Theatre and Performance in Africa: Intercultural Perspectives.* 220 pp. DM 39.-
32. *The Novels of Nuruddin Farah.* 170 pp. DM 29.- [DM 44,90 cloth]
33. *Échanges Franco-Allemands sur l'Afrique.* 252 pp. DM 39.-
34. *Contemporary Relativism with Reference to Culture and Africa.* 270 pp. DM 39.-
35. *Aids-Education through Theatre: Case Studies from Uganda.* 205 pp. DM 39.-
36. *Theatre for Development.* 80 pp. DM 14.90
37. *The Life and Writings of Gakaara wa Wanjau.* 276 pp. DM 39.-
38. *Primary Education and Social Integration.* 183 pp. DM 39.-
39. *Uganda: The Literary Landscape.* ca. 230 pp. 39.-
40. *Contemporary Nigerian Theatre.* 306 pp, 20 photographs. DM 44.90
41. *Land Law and Land Ownership in Africa.* 260 pp. DM 39.90
42. *Contemporary African Fiction.* 268 pp. DM 39.90
43. *Theatre and Popular Culture in Southern Africa.* ca. 220 pp. DM 29.90
44. *Blackness - Culture, Ideology, and Discourse.* 288 pp. DM 29.90
45. *Contemporary Nigerian Poetry and the Poetics of Orality.* 220 pp. DM 29.90
46. *The Legal Profession in Tanzania.* 350 pp. DM 44.90
47. *Nigerian Art Music.* 186 pp. DM 29.95
48. *Igbo Women Novelists: The Poetics of Orality or Poetics of "Writing Back"?.* ca. 385 pp. DM 44.95

(Prices do not include postage)

Bayreuth African Studies
ECKHARD BREITINGER

New and forthcoming titles
Spring/summer 2001

BASS 51
Ingrid Rissom (ed) *Languages in Contrast in East Africa*
268 pp; ISBN 3-927510-64-5 DM 39.90; Euro 19.99; £ 13.99 (Aug. 2001)

BASS 53
Gyimah Labi: *African Music Theory* 205 pp; *with accomp. CD*: ISBN 3-927510-62-9; DM 64.90; Euro 32.99; £ 17.99 (Oct. 2001)

BASS 54
Mongo Beti parle réalisée et editée par Ambroise Kom, pp 198, ISBN 3-927510-65-3 DM 29.90; Euro 14.99; £ 9.99, (Sept. 2001)

BASS 55
Tirop P. Simatei: *The Novel and the Politics of Nation Building in East Africa,* pp 189, ISBN 3-927510-70-X; DM 29.90; Euro 14.99; £ 9.99 (Feb. 2001)

BASS 56
Charles Bodunde (ed.) *Literatures in African Languages,* 268 pp. ISBN 3-927510-66-1; DM 39.90; Euro 19.99; £ 13.99 (Feb.2001)

BASS 57
Kyallo Wadi Wamitila: *Archetypal Criticism of Kiswahili Poetry,* pp 245, ISBN 3-927510-68-8; DM 39.90; Euro 19.99; £ 13.99 (May 2001)

BASS 58
Charles Bodunde: *Oral Traditions and Aesthetic Transfer —Form and Social Vision in Black Poetry,* pp 205; ISBN 3-927510-69-9, DM 29.90; Euro 14.99; £ 9.99 (April 2001)

BASS 59
Ulli Beier: *The Hunter thinks the Monkey is not wise..- Selected Essays,* ed. by Wole Ogundele, pp 264, ISBN 3-927510-71-8 DM 39.90; Euro 19.99; £ 13.99 (April 2001)

BASS 60
Oknomme Okome: (ed) *The Poetry of Tanure Ojaide,* ca 180 pp; ISBN 3-927510-67-X, ca. DM 29.90; Euro 14.99; £ 9.99 (October 2001)

e-mail: eckhard.breitinger@uni-bayreuth.de